Daughter of a Gun

Daughter of a Gun

Kaori Tanegashima

iUniverse, Inc.
New York Bloomington Shanghai

Daughter of a Gun

iUniverse books may be ordered through booksellers or by contacting:

iUniverse
1663 Liberty Drive
Bloomington, IN 47403
www.iuniverse.com
1-800-Authors (1-800-288-4677)

Because of the dynamic nature of the Internet, any Web addresses or links contained in this book may have changed since publication and may no longer be valid.

ISBN: 978-0-595-49914-4 (pbk)

ISBN: 978-0-595-61303-8 (ebk)

Printed in the United States of America

Contents

Acknowledgments

I am indebted to my family in Japan and the United States, and friends and students who encouraged me to write and waited impatiently for the results.

Special thanks go to Dr. Doris Eggert, who translated the manuscript into German and prepared it for publication in Europe.

Kudos for the cover design go to Mr. Tom Hofer, graphic artist for the Palisadian Post. The cover image of the "Tanegashima Matchlock" rifle is courtesy of Monte Schumacher.

I am grateful to my older brother Keiji Tanegashima for sharing his vivid memories of our life in China. I relied on his support and his contributions to fill in details.

The final push towards publication came from Mr. Charles W. Shirriff, a fellow author and the husband of my lifelong pen pal Wilma Shirriff.

Preface

In Japan the name, Tanegashima, is synonymous with guns. A *Chronicle of Guns (Teppooki)*, written by my ancestor Tokitaka, the 14th Lord of the Island of Tanegashima south of the main islands of Japan, tells the story of the Portuguese captain who became shipwrecked with his crew on Tanegashima Island in the year 1543. The Portuguese sought refuge with the Japanese inhabitants of the island, who had never seen Westerners before, nor had they ever seen firearms. The young Lord Tokitaka was fascinated.

One of many sagas written, and later even made into movies, says that when 1000 pieces of gold would not persuade the Portuguese captain to part with one of his rifles, Tokitaka traded Wakasa, the beautiful daughter of a famous sword smith, for one of the mysterious weapons. Legend has it that the captain's and Wakasa's union was the first interracial marriage between a Westerner and a Japanese and that it produced the first mixed-blood child. Perhaps more importantly, this is when and how guns were introduced to Japan. Within one year mega shoguns were fighting their wars with these new and more powerful weapons now produced in Japan.

I am a direct descendant of Tokitaka Tanegashima. In Japanese I would also be described as a *Teppoo musume,* a daughter of a gun. However, a literal translation into English is a daughter who leaves and never returns like a bullet leaving the barrel of a gun. That is the story of my life.

PHOTOGRAPH

Signature of Bearer

種子島かほり

所　持　人　自　署

1

It Shall Be A Boy!

 I do not remember the day of my birth. However, I have heard it described by members of my family so many times that it has become part of my memories, the earliest one, so to speak.

A mood of confident expectancy pervaded the family mansion, a compound of several buildings forming a private fortress, close to the Summer Palace and the North Sea Park neighborhood of Old Beijing. The year was 1939. Another baby, the fourth for Juro and Tane Tanegashima was about to be born. All signs were good. The mother had been carrying low and her stomach was big.

The midwife, with a life of experiences behind her, proclaimed, "It shall be a boy!"

There were already two daughters and a boy. Another daughter would be a burden. Another boy would strengthen the position of the mother as wife and matriarch. A wife so successful need not fear divorce for committing one of the seven sins women in many Asian societies could be charged with.

By the time my father came home, I had been delivered. The atmosphere throughout the house had changed. My father immediately sensed that something was wrong. Mother and midwife avoided his eyes. He inspected his new child. "No *chimpo!*" he shouted. For a long time he will introduce his new baby daughter to his drinking buddies as "my other son, who is missing something in front." That is how I, Kaori Tanegashima, entered this world. As we grew up, my two older sisters wore kimonos and were taught to do the traditional girl things. I grew up in the hand-me-down clothes of my older brother and was often mistaken for a boy. I learned to play rough. One day I overheard my older sister telling my mother that this big boy in our neighborhood had hit her. I found a stick, went after that boy and hit him over the head.

When his mother came to complain, my mother looked at me and said, "How could a little girl like her put such a big bump on such a big boy's head?"

This is the earliest memory I have of myself as a defender of the weak.

In Japanese culture from childhood on, group activity and decision-making are stressed by all major institutions, with schools being the most powerful. I was subjected to this enormous pressure like everyone else. However, for reasons I could not have explained at the time, I reacted differently even before I entered grade school. I was about four years old when my older sisters and brother were enrolled in a Japanese school, which was part of the expatriate Japanese community. Our *ahma* packed *bentoo* (box lunch) for each of them and off they went. I insisted that I get a *bentoo*, also, and marched off to school with the others. On rainy days, we rode a Chinese rickshaw called *yanchoo*. At the school, I would stand outside the classroom windows listening and memorizing what was taught inside. With what I learned, I became the "teacher" of my preschool peers, the other Japanese children in our neighborhood. I made little "textbooks" from pieces of scrap paper and ordered them to memorize the characters I had written onto them. By the time I entered school myself I was accustomed to being the one that all the others turned to for advice, leadership and protection. My efforts to make fun and games for my "students," were appreciated by their parents.

My small world in which I played a large role came crashing down when my younger sister Chisato was born. Suddenly, all the attention seemed to be on her. My mother adored and preferred her to me, or so I thought. To make things worse, Chisako developed into an exceptionally bright and precocious child as though she had been born mature. Adults took to her naturally and vice versa. Every time she was praised, which to me seemed to be all the time, I hated her. Often I wished she were dead. I let her fall from my back, when I was supposed to carry her, made her gasp for air dropping a silk cloth over her face. Yet later, when she was barely four years old and we had returned to Japan, she would do my school homework, while I sneaked outside to play.

One day, my older sister called me home from school. She said Chisato had died.

"You killed her, because you hated her," she hissed.

I felt like sinking deeper with each step I took in the snow as we walked home together. No one knew the brain disease that took Chisato's life. But I knew that I had killed her with my vicious wishes and petty jealousies. At her funeral, I thought all eyes were on me. No one comforted me. My mother was inconsolable. She was determined to replace Chisato with another child.

It is said, and scientific studies seem to confirm, that the expectations those around you have of you and your behavior strongly influence who you are and how you behave. If this is so, my father's expectations of his "second son with something missing in front" both restricted and liberated me in ways most other children growing up in Japanese society cannot experience. The restrictions had to do with my being different. No child wants to be clearly different. However, with the tacit support of my father I learned to live with it and to turn it to my advantage.

One day many years later, my father looked at me and said, "You should have been my son. You are the strong one."

For a Japanese father to say this to his daughter was most unusual. For a Japanese daughter to receive such an extraordinary compliment from anyone was rare indeed. For me it was a defining moment. Being different from my female peers was all right.

There were many attempts to change me. Among those who tried were the other members of my family whom I often embarrassed with my unorthodox and headstrong behavior.

The time when my stepmother learned to apologize to her friends for my faux pas by screaming, "She's an American! What can you expect?" had not arrived, as yet.

My teachers tried their luck, too. One teacher in elementary school felt deeply sorry for me because I was the only female student with a name that did not end in *ko*. She called me *Kaori-ko-san*. But I loved my name. It means fragrance, and it re-enforced beautifully, I thought, my being different. Occasionally, my name led to fortuitous mistakes. Once I won an essay contest, because the judges assumed I was a boy. Gender discrimination was and still is common in Japan. I had always been aware of it, but fancied myself immune to its sting and able to deal with it until the day of my high school graduation.

On that day, the honor of being the valedictorian went to the student with the highest grade point average. I was that student. A girl had never been valedictorian. In what I considered then and still consider today abject cowardice and corruption, my school officials decided that a girl should not represent the graduating class. They changed some of my grades so that a boy would come out ahead. My father in an unusual public support of a daughter's rights, tried to intervene. To no avail. *Shikata ga nai*, it cannot be helped, there is no way to change the situation. I flew into a rage. However, showing strong emotions either of affection or of dislike are regarded as very bad behavior in Japanese culture and are not easily tolerated. You will be marked a troublemaker, one who disturbs the harmony of the group.

Japanese magazines are now full of *romansu,* and there is incessant talk about changes under way in Japanese culture. However, resistance to change is, indeed, a hallmark of this culture. Whatever changes have occurred and are purportedly now under way, their pace is incremental rather than revolutionary, superficial rather than fundamental. This holds true for about 40% of young Japanese men and women, who still rely on go-betweens to arrange suitable matches.

My parent's marriage had been arranged. Bride and groom had not known each other before and had no romantic feelings for each other. That was the rule. There were few exceptions. What counted was that a "right" match according to family status and lineage would be achieved. My mother was an only child. In this case, the object of an arranged marriage was to carry on the family name. My father was co-opted and "adopted" to take on the name Tanegashima in order to continue the line. He did his duty siring six children. But he also felt justified in having extramarital affairs from time to time. Later, when we learned in my biology class in high school about the higher potential for inheriting deformities and even insanity from unions of close relatives, my father, with the help of a considerable amount of *sake*, confided to me that he was, indeed, a first cousin of my mother. Moreover, their parents, my grand parents, had been first cousins, too. That, my father explained, was a common practice to make the bloodline purer.

My father had lived in China as a single man for more than fifteen years after he was graduated at the top of his class from Shimonoseki Business School, located in Yamaguchi Prefecture in the Southwest of Honshu Island. He had been recruited by the Manchurian Railroad Company, a part of the *Zaibatsu*, the Japanese system of commercial enterprises tightly interlocking and intertwined with Japanese banks and the government bureaucracy in mutually supportive and beneficial, and often corrupt, relationships. The *Zeibatsu* provided the economic power, drive and organizational backing for Japan's stunning military expansion starting at the turn of the 20th century. The company sent my father to Dairen, China, to continue his college training before welcoming the now elite scholar to their accounting department. His rise to chief clerk was only temporarily interrupted when he was ordered to return to Japan to marry my mother. Together they returned to Beijing. He spent another fifteen years there. Those were good and carefree years. Family and fortune grew.

Our life in Beijing as privileged occupying foreigners was pleasant. We lived in a walled and fenced in community with other Japanese around us. Our house was one of the old Beijing style houses. Few of them are left in their original condition. They provide too much space for too few people in a nation with a population of 1.3 billion. Typically, such a house had a main building at the back of the complex. Subsidiary wings ran along two sides housing maids' quarters, kitchen, guest and service rooms. Inside, the floors were covered with what the Chinese called *Anpera carpet* and we called *goza*, tightly woven mats made from fine reeds or straw. They covered the raw earth underneath. On top of the *goza* the Japanese would often put their *tatami* mats.

A simple, forbidding white wall broken by the entrance and a line of small windows formed the front to the street. The windows were made of attractive geometric latticework and pasted over with fine white paper. In Beijing these houses were single story, gray or white brick buildings with tiled roofs and woodwork painted dark red. The buildings enclosed a large courtyard where trees and vines provided shade in the summer heat. I did not know it then, but geomancy, known in China as *feng shui*, meaning wind and water, had been important when the house we lived in was built. Geomancy is the practice of building houses in harmony with the earth's vital energy. This is to assure good health and good fortune for the occupier. It dates back thousands of years and is still widely practiced today. First written records mentioning geomancy appear during the Han dynasty (206 BC-AD 220). A geomancer works with a special *feng shui* compass in order to determine the correct position of a building on a proposed site. He must consider topography, type of ground, surrounding landscape, nearby rivers and other water sources, as well as the direction the building faces. Together these factors make up the *chi* or the energy of the site. In the countryside, but even in cities to an extent, geomancy has often led to a breathtakingly beautiful integration of houses into their natural setting. Whether or not our house benefited much from geomancy, I cannot say. However, there was a great sense of harmony and being sheltered and protected when we lived there.

Our household included several female servants called *ahmas*. Like nuns devoting their lives to Christ, *ahmas* did not expect to marry, but served one family all their lives. Each *ahma* was assigned special duties. My brother and sisters had one *ahma* each to call their own. The youngest, whom we called Hanako, was assigned to me. She was 18 years old. One day she pleaded with my mother not to call her Hanako, because it meant beggar in Chinese. From then on, she became Hana-chan, meaning, "flower dear."

When I was a baby, Hana-chan would strap me on her back while doing other duties. Later, when I could talk and walk, I begged her to take me along to the local markets. The Chinese market and the stores were outside our walled-in Japanese community. It was dangerous for us to venture outside. The Chinese did not like us. They were mostly poor and resentful of the foreigners living in their midst. We Japanese, who had borrowed liberally from the early superior Chinese culture for centuries, had been indoctrinated to treat the local Chinese population as backward and low-class.

Once in a while a vendor would come by just outside the gate to hawk freshly steamed buns.

"*Santoo, mantoo!*" he chanted like a mantra.

Mimicking his calls, I would rush out and follow his cart to the entrance gate. I can still smell, taste, and feel the lovely buns that looked and felt like my mother's breasts. The times that my *ahma* took me to the Chinese market I would come home flushed with excitement and pride. Every time I had learned new Chinese words, all of them bad. Chinese children would come up against the fence surrounding our compound. We screamed bad Japanese words at them. It did not take them long to scream them back at us. Now, behind my mother's back, I was able to use my newly acquired Chinese fighting vocabulary.

One day my mother heard me. "Where did you learn those dirty words?"

My excursions to the market were revealed. *Ahma* was scolded and forbidden to take me out ever again.

On a different level, my father involved himself in teaching us manners and ethics, too.

Maybe once a week, for example, he would do a ritual cleansing of the family sword in front of all his children. Moving with quiet deliberation, using a small cloth ball filled with white powder, he would begin by dusting the sharp blade. "Pong, pong, pong" bounced the little cloth ball before my father dropped it and began slowly polishing the sword from top to bottom, all the while giving us an occasional deadly serious look but not saying a word. We tried to conceal our rising fear. When the sword gleamed like the sun, my father carefully wrapped the middle part of it leaving the sharp tip exposed.

"This is what I will have to do if one of you throws mud on our family name," he would say, going through the motions of a Samurai committing *harakiri*.

Our grandmother had her own fear-inspiring ritual. Following an ancient Chinese and Japanese remedy, she would burn *moxa,* a downy material made from a variety of dried plants, between her thumb and index finger. This was to cure her arthritis and left an unsightly black scab. One day I broke one of my father's favorite and prized blue and white Ming vases. As I was fleeing from the scene of the crime, I passed my grandmother, who was giving herself her daily *moxa* treatment. The smell was terrible, but I was more afraid of her giving me the treatment as a punishment, too.

"Oh, here you are! What are you up to?" she asked, keeping her eyes on the burning *moxa*.

"Nothing. I'm going to play outside," I mumbled as I ran away from her.

"Come back before dark, you hear!"

Once outside, I ran to the big pear tree in our courtyard and took off my shoes. I left them neatly at the bottom before climbing up to hide. For a long time, endless it seemed to me, no one came to look for me. I struggled to stay awake.

Finally I heard my *ahma* cry out, "*Aiii*!!!" when she discovered where her charge was hiding and I told her why.

"What shall I tell your father?"

But after she had coaxed me down from the tree, and my father heard what had happened, he did not mention the broken vase at all. He did not need to. His *harakiri* "lessons" had been enough.

My older brother and sisters went to a Japanese school where they were taught to speak proper Mandarin Chinese. I was not yet in school and had no way of telling street from polite language. However, the effect I had on the Chinese kids screaming at them in their own bad vocabulary was my first lesson in the power of language. No matter how inappropriate my mother might find the words I used, this lesson stayed with me all my life.

After we had returned to Japan, I discovered that speaking a language different from the one used around you to be a handicap. Using Chinese words alerted the other schoolchildren to our being "foreigners." They called us names and threw stones.

"Best not to speak Chinese," my father said. "Better to pick up the local dialect as quickly as possible!"

I added Nagasaki dialect as protective coating. Every time we moved to a new prefecture after that, I had to pick up another dialect to fit in. Finally, in boarding school, I could return to the standard Tokyo speech I had spoken in China. In that school it was the only "dialect" everybody understood.

While still in China, I learned other unladylike skills. For example, trapping sparrows with a bamboo basket resting on one chopstick with a string attached over rice sprinkled underneath. As the birds ducked in to pick the rice, I pulled the string to bring down the basket over them. I also hunted birds with stones and a sling shot. *Ahma* would pluck their feathers and marinade the meat, while my father enjoyed sipping *sake* as the birds were barbecued. The preparation and his eating of the birds I had caught fascinated and shocked me. To this day, I cannot eat sparrows and pigeons served in Chinese restaurants. The Chinese have a way to prepare as food almost anything that grows or moves. One must take a Chinese menu literally. If it features "birds' nests," it will be birds' nests. This delighted my father and disgusted the rest of us.

My grandmother lived with us. Uncles and aunts were close by. Other Japanese relatives came to work in the Manchurian Railroad Company. Servants ran the household and cared for the children. Through all this, my mother moved like a queen. My father would take us out for dinner. Once I made a fuss insisting that I wanted to eat just one course. Money was plentiful. There was a measure of social freedom that came with being part of the occupying forces. In those days in Japan, for example, a husband going out with his wife would be unheard of. Even today, this is more the exception than the rule.

Most children remember the simple lullabies their mothers, nurses or maids sang to them. For me it was the clicking of Mah Jongg tiles. My father was an avid player. Two or three times a week, he and his male friends would gather at our house to play deep into the night. No women in the room, of course, except for the maid serving *sake* and *surume*, dried squid. I loved to count the sticks with different designs, which are used to tally up the amounts of money lost or won. I loved the atmosphere of quiet concentration, broken by sudden shouts of joy or exaggerated despair, and the good-natured ribbing between the players. Many a night the clicking tiles rocked me to sleep. As soon as we were old enough, my father inducted us as players. On New Year's Day he would give us *otoshidama,* small amounts of lucky money to play with against him. We knew very soon, that he would probably win it all back, but we were hooked. I still am.

From time to time, our house would fill with strangers. On one occasion there were Russian Jews fleeing Stalin's purges. Of course, I did not know this. We communicated in sign language and by singing. Dressed in our best kimono, we children were pressed into entertaining the visitors with songs. Broad smiles and loud clapping were our rewards. I still love to sing. Even when I am very sad, singing relieves my pain and unhappiness.

My mother concerned herself with our education, taught us manners and supervised the domestic helpers. No one taught my mother how to deal with adversity or how to survive. That would turn out to be the tragedy of her life and change the lives of everyone in our family.

Meanwhile, our lives were surprisingly peaceful, in fact, stunningly so. Two years before the end of the war, we moved from Beijing to Tsingtao, the Green Island, formerly occupied by Germany. The one, and probably only, popular part of the Germans' legacy was the now famous Tsingtao beer sold worldwide. Tsingtao is a resort near the sea, where the wealthy come to vacation.

Our protected, comfortable and almost idyllic life ended in 1945, as World War II was drawing to a close.

Officials of the Chinese Nationalist government made my father an offer: "Stay and help us build a new country. If you do, your family will be safe and your money and other assets will not be confiscated."

The alternative was to leave all his possessions and money and take his wife and five children back to a most uncertain future in Japan. While my father sat up through the nights agonizing about what to do, events began to narrow his choices. Japanese colleagues from his company and some of our neighbors were blacklisted and arrested as enemy foreigners. Some of their wives and children came to hide in our house. Chinese hatred and determination for revenge for crimes and atrocities committed by the Japanese Army in China ran high. The distinction between Japanese soldiers and Japanese civilians living in China was lost. Now, whenever we had to go outside our compound, our Chinese employees and domestic helpers would surround us to protect us from "outside" Chinese. Everywhere there were armed guards in front of public buildings. We were ordered to bow as we passed.

"Bend down and pretend you are picking something up," my mother whispered setting an example for us to follow.

One day in December of 1945 a heavy army truck rumbled down the street and came to a stop in front of our house. Japan had lost the war and signed an unconditional surrender. From the south had come the victorious Chinese with their American liberators.

They shouted, "Defeat! All Japanese must leave China!"

We would have to return to our domicile of origin, the last permanent address our family had was in Japan before coming to China.

Before the truck arrived, we had watched in silence as Chinese officials went through our house red tagging everything we owned. Thus were the contents of the house, including my father's large and precious jade collection, made off-limits to us, to be divided among the new and "rightful" owners. Later, we left with little more than the clothes we wore. At the port, soldiers searched our bodies and took whatever caught their fancy. They took my mother's wedding ring, my treasured jade abacus and my sister's favorite doll. Some of the other Japanese women carried pillowcases stuffed with rice and beans. Some were able to get those past the guards. Such survival tricks would never have occurred to my mother. We were the ones to arrive in Japan with pillowcases filled with buckwheat chaff. As the ship pulled out of the harbor, our dog was wailing on the dock.

The voyage on an American war ship from Tsingtao to Sasebo harbor lasted three days. The ship had no cabins, only large empty windowless holds where each family was assigned a certain area. We spread straw mats on the floor and blankets on top to sit and sleep there. Japanese prisoners of war served us Japanese food. Americans manned and operated the vessel. They treated us, their enemy cargo, with shocking civility. Wild rumors traded as facts had prepared us for the worst; American GIs would cut out our tongues, if we spoke to them. Don't accept chewing gum or chocolate, they are poisoned! Girls pretend to be boys! Curiosity soon got the better of us. "*Haroo*" (Hello!) we children would scream at the Americans, and then run away quickly. The Americans returned our furtive greetings with easy, good-natured smiles. We had never seen other human beings walk, talk, and act with such open and casual self-confidence. However, it was the warm directness, the genuine concern so many GI's wore on their sleeves, and above all their radiant smiles that touched us and made us forget the dire warnings.

2

Going Across The Sea

✦

Umi Yukaba

Our ship docked at Hariojima Island in Nagasaki Prefecture. We were all given painful injections and quarantined on board. There was an outbreak of infectious disease on land. But after only three days, American navy men took us ashore to an assembly center, where we joined other returnees. No one came to greet us. We made our way to my mother's relatives in Ainoura, a part of Sasebo City. By and by, we found other relatives in the area. It was not a happy homecoming. The proverbial Japanese hospitality was stretched beyond reasonable limits. Sasebo is very close to Nagasaki, which had been destroyed by an atomic bomb six months before our arrival, killing an estimated 120,000 people. Survivors had flooded surrounding communities. Refugees from Nagasaki and Japanese returnees from lands formerly occupied by Japan were assigned into houses still standing, very much against the wishes of the owners. Some of our relatives had taken over my mother's share of inheritances during our absence. This was legal in Japan. Absentee ownership was not recognized or protected. What the relatives had not acquired had been taken by the government. Some of the Sasebo government buildings had, in fact, been built on our land.

Our sudden return was a mortifying embarrassment and our presence at a time of severe shortages an intolerable burden. We were six unwanted relatives at my mother's cousin's house. Worse, we did not come prepared to accept graciously the catastrophic fall that we had taken.

When our host served us a meal of rice blackened by seaweed, my oldest sister Fusako, ever so much the lady our mother had tried to teach her to be, took one look, raised her eyebrows and said categorically, "I don't eat things like that."

For reasons I cannot explain other than my strong instinct for survival, I did not share this attitude. I sensed that our survival was indeed at stake. I ate everything and soon became one of the "providers" for the family.

Our stay at the relatives was difficult and unpleasant. Still, nothing could have prepared us for what followed. My father had founded a support group to help evacuees and returnees. He had seen to it that four barracks, "residences" formerly housing women factory workers, were made available to us. We moved into one of the jail cell type rooms lining both sides of long corridors. Our room had a door to the corridor on one side, and a window and outlet at the other end, which opened onto a handkerchief-sized, totally bare, fenced in piece of solid ground. Communal kitchens were in the middle of the barracks. At one end of the corridors, laundry was done in cold water in cement basins. This is where later, barely nine years old, I would wash diapers in freezing water. Communal toilets, a horror and affront to our sense of privacy, were at the other end of the building.

There were more complications. Our long stay abroad had turned us into foreigners in our own land, where nothing is more important than to fit in with the group, with the people around you. Not a hint of being different would be tolerated. That would bring forth the natural cruelty in children as well as the only slightly more restrained hatred of the adults. Later I would learn that this attitude is one of the most characteristic parts of Japanese culture and is not necessarily related to good or bad times.

Our new Japanese neighbors resented us further, because they believed that we had sat out the war in comfort in China, while they suffered through massive bombing raids and hunger. That was mostly true. Nationalist China had been on the side of the allies and no systematic bombing took place. We did have blackouts and routine runs into bomb shelters while B29 bombers flew overhead. In the cold and clammy shelters, my oldest sister would keep us quiet telling ghost stories that scared us more than the bombers flying overhead.

One thing our Japanese neighbors could not know was the patriotic demeanor required of Japanese living abroad. Every day my mother checked the newspaper to see if the Japanese emperor's picture might be on or in it, before handing the paper to the maids to wrap up fish and groceries. To use the paper with the emperor's picture on it for such mundane purposes could bring arrest and a charge of treason. We demonstrated our loyalty singing songs dedicated to the Imperial Family. Once my oldest sister won a contest and was chosen to sing on a radio broadcast to Japan. Radio was then the only wireless means of mass communication. My sister being on it was a sensation. The whole family gathered around the set to listen to her sing, *"Umi Yukaba,"* (Going across the sea). I did not understand the meaning of the lyrics, but my sister's voice is still clear in my mind.

Now there were seven of us in one small container room. Lack of privacy in Japanese society is common. This was extreme. Nevertheless, like everyone else around us, we soon became expert in creating private spaces where there were none. If one of us had to change clothes or undress and wash up, the others instinctively turned their backs. For a moment, one was "alone." In small Japanese homes, paper screens and doors provide an illusion of privacy. On public transportation and in public places, people will themselves to be alone, creating a private sphere around them on the most crowded trains.

The lack of privacy we learned to deal with. The lack of food was another matter. Food was rationed, but the allotted amounts were not enough to keep us alive. There were severe shortages of everything basic, which made ration coupons and paper money worthless. Barter on the Black Market almost totally replaced a money economy. For this, my mother was ill prepared. Besides, what did she have to barter? By and by, she traded her lovely kimonos for sacks of potatoes and other food. But it was not even a real trade, because the farmers were sick and tired of city people's fine wares that they had no use for in their daily chores.

"What are we to do with your fancy kimonos?"

"Keep them for your daughters' weddings," my mother pleaded.

Even if successful, there was another problem—how to get the sacks of potatoes or whatever through the inspections of the food guards at the railroad stations. If caught, everything my mother was carrying would be confiscated. We children had a strategy worked out. We would hang around the station awaiting my mother's arrival. As soon as we spied her getting off the train, we would rush in to create a scene to distract the guards. My mother with a sack of potatoes strapped to her back disguised as a baby with a baby's cap on top then made her way through the gate while we were still harassing the "enemy." Then, as soon as we were home, another challenge—the neighbors, as though they could smell the potatoes, would come to our door to beg for their share.

"We have no kimono, nothing to trade for food," they said, enough to make my mother give up some of her precious loot.

I hated this and my father thought it was stupid to act that way. It was also a generosity my sickly and malnourished mother could ill afford.

In these circumstances one day my older sister, my brother and I were stuffed into a closet, while our sister, Megumi, was born. We were intensely curious and tried our luck one by one squinting through a crack in the closet door. However, there was little we could see. There was much running back and forth, noises we had never heard before, until finally there was the cry of the newborn baby. Three months later my mother died from hunger and exhaustion. I was eight and a half years old. No one explained to me why my mother had died. At the funeral, my mother was laid out for us to say good-bye. Without warning, her body was rolled into the crematorium and burned.

To this day, I want to scream at the thought, as I screamed then, "Why do you burn my mother? Stop it!"

Instead, my father carried me out of the room and made me wait alone in the hearse.

The death of my mother changed all our lives. My oldest sister, Fusako, had just graduated from high school and had been accepted to Kurume Women's College, a reputable medical school. Her dream was to become a medical doctor. Now she became a substitute mother for four siblings and a three-month-old baby. My father, true to Japanese tradition, could not be counted on to help raise the children, let alone do any kind of housework. That was a concept absent from Japanese culture until very recently.

My job became to wash the baby's diapers and search for a nursing mother. I hated it. School was my escape. I took the longest way home for which my sister-mother duly scolded me. I missed playing with the neighborhood kids and dreaded every moment of the baby's crying. The baby cried a lot. We had no milk. I was sent out to find some. With the baby strapped on my back, I walked from door to door listening for babies crying. I would knock on the door. If a mother with a baby on her arm opened, I would beg for her to share her milk with my baby sister. Many of the mothers looked as malnourished as my mother had been. Few were ready to share what little they had. Often I wished I could leave the baby on someone's doorstep and walk away. Other "baby food" I gathered were oysters if I could find them on the rocks by the sea. Fresh raw oysters, I found to my surprise, my infant sister loved to slurp.

One day there were no oysters and no mother's milk. A farmer working his small rice field nearby found us sitting by the wayside crying.

"Why are you crying?" he asked.

"We have nothing to eat," I wailed.

The farmer listened and thought for a while.

"Do you know how to massage my back? It is the planting of the rice seedlings—it's killing me."

Massage his back? I stopped crying.

One thing my father had taught me how to do was *shiatsu*, an acupressure technique, and he had also shown me how to massage his back by walking on it barefoot. The farmer and I struck a deal—goat milk and eggs for "treatments." Then he had an even better idea; he would let me have one of his goats so I could use its milk for the baby. I learned that goats give milk and you can actually drink it. The only other milk I had known until then was mother's milk. Cow's milk was not then sold in stores or markets in Japan. I learned to milk the goat. I massaged the farmer's back and took home eggs as payment. Soon he let me have two chickens to complete my farm in the tiny garden plot outside our container room. Goat and chicken had to be fed, but I preferred the gathering of feed for them to begging for food. At age nine, I was now a major provider in the family.

My days of going door to door, however, were not over yet. One of my older sisters had found a job in a factory, packing cheap chocolate pellets into small containers. She took me along to help. We were paid next to nothing but our boss explained that we could make lots more money if we sold the packaged chocolate door to door. I revisited all the houses where I had begged for milk and food before. This time my reception was as close to cordial as Japanese can get and there were smiles and bows all around. No one offered money. They all thought I had come to show my appreciation for their former kindness. There was nothing I could do but smile and bow back.

3

Perfect Liberty

After our return from China, one of my mother's dearest friends, Mrs. Maeda, was one of the few people who tried to help us get settled and survive. One day she asked my parents to come with her to a church north of Sasebo. It was one of the houses of worship of the religious sect, Perfect Liberty, (PL), then rising to prominence. Until then organized religion had not played much of a role in our lives. Ancestor worship, filial piety and nature appreciation were part of our lives, but they were also part of Japanese culture in general. Our home had a family Buddhist altar with our ancestor tablets in a corner of our living room. There we made ceremonial food offerings and Buddhist monks occasionally conducted commemorative services. For us children this was a fascinating ritual. It had little to do with believing in God. In fact, the concept of one God exclusionary of all other Gods is foreign to the Japanese.

Perfect Liberty is the modern incarnation of the former *Hito no michi*—the People's Way, founded before the Second World War. That sect then had attracted millions of members. The Japanese military government perceived it and other sects as a threat to emperor worship and unquestioned patriotism. The sects' leaders were arrested and imprisoned and their organizations dissolved. After the war General MacArthur in his role as the temporary *tennoo heika*, the emperor of the defeated nation, had religious freedom written into the new Japanese constitution. The real emperor Hirohito was no longer to be worshiped as a God. The door was thrown open to new and old religions and sects of all kinds. Many rushed in to fill the many spiritual and practical needs of a nation in desperation, confusion and deep shock.

Our needs were mostly of the practical kind. My mother was sick and dying. My father had lost his fortune and position. The family was starving. PL promised a way out of this misery. My father began to attend daily early morning meetings at the PL church. He came to agree with the doctrine of the church based on twenty-one declarations starting with "Life is Art," and a collection of more or less common sense, but no moral, imperatives comparable to the biblical Ten Commandments. Rather, these declarations by the Holy Father mounted on large tablets on the walls were meant as a primer on how to live by the rules of PL.

Life for us was still a long way from being art. My father was trying to feed his family collecting scrap metal and melting it down to make it into a variety of utensils for which little need existed. When this business failed miserably, he worked as an accountant for PL. Over two years he built up a reputation for loyalty. One day the second pastor of PL in Sasebo asked my father to become a pastor. There was an opening at the headquarters of PL in Shimizu City in Shizuoka Prefecture. Apparently, no rigorous special training or years of studying scriptures were required. Loyalty and a willingness to sacrifice oneself and, perhaps more important, all of one's assets, was sufficient. After my mother's death, my father and two of my sisters, the oldest and the youngest, moved into quarters on what was, and is, essentially a closed community owned and controlled by PL. My brother, one older sister and I were put into separate PL dormitories, but attended regular public schools.

Two years after my mother died, my father remarried. Again, it was an arranged marriage, this time arranged by the boss of our future stepmother. She, like my father's first wife, had very little to say in the matter. A woman was needed to take care of my baby sister and relieve my father and oldest sister of the household duties. It was a contract for all-around services that the new wife was expected to perform without question or protest.

The woman, who was to become our stepmother, was 13 years younger than my father. I now recognize from old photographs that she was also beautiful. When she came into our lives, we did not see her as beautiful in any way. She intruded into our territory. Our defenses went up. A tug-of-war began that would last until we were all far beyond adulthood. In that, our stepmother was a strong and eminently capable opponent. An adversary relationship developed because of the general inability of Japanese to communicate frankly and openly with each other. Not until many years later, for example, did I learn about my new mother's traumatic earlier experiences during the war. In an earlier marriage, she had been the servant of the husband's family who, among many other indignities, had made her stay in their house alone during the bombing raids on Tokyo.

We fought mostly over territory. The "second mother's" first and major move was to keep all older siblings in the dormitories, but raise baby sister Megumi as her own at home. My older brother, sister, and I felt abandoned.

I wrote my father a letter, "Why have you abandoned me? Why do you never come to visit me? Why am I the one who never gets any mail?"

When he came by a few days later, we sat and talked. Neither he nor I mentioned my letter. I noticed that a button was loose on his coat.

"Let me sew on that button," I said.

As I was sewing, my father smoked a cigarette and looked out the window.

"My eyesight isn't as good as it used to be. I could use a little reading lamp," I said into the silence.

A few days later a little lamp was delivered to me. I cherished it throughout my dormitory life. We learned to cope and to develop what I later learned Americans call a thick skin. Summer vacations were particularly trying. It was the only time when we had to be home for one month because the school dormitories were closed. Our new mother seemed to take pains to let us know what a financial burden we were to her. To this day when we have family gatherings and enough *sake* has loosened our tongues, a reservoir of childhood resentments breaks open and harsh words and lots of tears flow freely. True to Japanese custom, however, by early next morning polite behavior returns and we all go on as though the previous night's eruption had never taken place.

I was going on ten when I was sent to the dormitory for elementary school age children of PL employees in Hamamatsu City. It is impossible to live in Japan without being reasonably well disciplined and organized. But now my life became totally regimented, every moment of our lives was planned in advance. Committees did the planning and enforcing of rules, regulations and schedules. I became conditioned to predetermined signals over which I had no control. We slept six girls to a room, always with our pleated skirts neatly folded under our futon beds on the floor.

At four o'clock in the morning, a bell with the force of a fire alarm rang to wake us. We folded our futons into closets, got dressed, and assembled for roll call in the one large room in the house, which also served as an assembly hall for a variety of other purposes. After roll call, while still sitting at attention on the floor facing a large picture of Tokuchika Miki, founder of PL, we would greet him with, "Good Morning, Holy Father!"

From an accordion-style Shinto prayer book in front of us we read aloud in unison: "We are born in this world as children of (Shinto) Gods ... We wish to ask for guidance on how to live our lives ... We ask for the blessing and protection of *kami*...."

After a brief ritual that involved certain hand motions resembling a cheerleader's routine, we bowed our heads in silent prayer. This is where I usually fell asleep and had to be nudged awake for the final singing of the PL anthem that ended this part of our early morning devotionals.

Still hours before breakfast, we would now report to our assigned stations for "*misasage,*" spiritual cleansing labor. Rotating specific duties from day to day, we cleaned our rooms, the common areas including the yard outside and the toilets. This done, we reassembled for "confessionals." Rather than admitting to sins, we were expected to share with each other how cleaning the toilets, for example, had enlightened us and made us spiritually stronger. In line with this character-building regimen, we were to take it in stride that there was no heat in our dormitory rooms during winter. We warmed up in front of the stove in the assembly room then ran back to crawl into our icy beds.

Finally, the time had come for *asa gohan*, the morning meal. Typically, this would consist of a bowl of rice and miso soup with pickles occasionally. Several containers with rice were spaced strategically to serve six to eight students sitting on both sides of long tables. The first day, on my best behavior, I ate slowly chewing every grain of rice before swallowing as I had been taught. When I reached for seconds, the rice container was empty. Modesty was not the best policy here. I learned to eat quickly. There was another reason for eating as fast as possible. The sooner we finished eating the more "free" time we had to play. That was the only time of the day, after meals, when we had some time to ourselves, though still in groups, of course. To this day, to the consternation of my family and friends, I usually outrace everyone at the table.

Once in school we traded the regimentation at our PL dormitory for the severe discipline of the public schools. After six hours of classes interrupted by a one-hour lunch break, we reported back to our dormitory for two hours of homework. At 4 p.m., we assembled once more to clean the dormitory. Then came cleaning up ourselves. This meant taking *ofuro,* the Japanese hot soaking baths, which were separated for boys and girls. Afterwards we hand-washed our underwear and hung it on a line. Finally, it was time for dinner. We looked forward to this, but more with interest than happy anticipation. Would there be some fish? Some meat even? But the fare was generally bland and basic. Fifty stomachs had to be filled. That was the chore of the housemothers. To tickle our palates was not high on their list of priorities. After dinner, we studied some more until evening prayers. By 9 p.m., the lights would be turned off. In the dark, now in our futon beds, we whispered and some of us, like me, read books by flashlight under the covers.

Our seven-day weeks were thus almost completely programmed for us. Input into planning or execution of schedules from us students was minimal or nonexistent with one exception. One Sunday a month, on what we called, "No-bell Day," we were more or less allowed to do what we wanted. The emphasis was on less. The prayers and cleaning could not be skipped. Leaving the premises required signing in and out. Most of us had no money to escape very far. But worst of all, this privilege could and was often taken away as punishment for breaking any of hundreds of rules.

The rules started with no crying in front of others. There was to be no complaining about anything, no criticizing nor defiance of authority. No makeup. No deviation from the uniform dress code. No curling of hair. Walking and running in a straight line only. No faking of illness to sleep in, which was my greatest temptation. No bad mouthing. No fighting. The list went on. It was based on the cultural imperative to obey authority willingly, enthusiastically and without question in the interest of living in harmony. Most of the rules and regulations we had to follow concerned possible infractions or trespasses that in Western culture would be understood as completely normal behavior of teenagers.

I am often asked if there was or is any room in Japanese schools for individual creativity and initiative. I am inclined to believe that if you are destined to be different, there are possibilities, severely limited though they might be. By destined I mean that if you were born into a different environment, had more energy, had the support of family or friends. In short, that there were specific reasons and events in your life that combined to make you understand and accept yourself as different from the crowd.

If I needed such proof of my being different, it came the first day at the dormitory. Somehow, the older students sensed that they had to teach me a lesson in submissiveness. They invited me to the lumberyard behind the dormitory.

"You are a *namaiki!*"—(impertinent)—they screamed and beat me up.

I was completely unprepared and stunned. Up to then, I had always been the one in control of the neighborhood children wherever we lived. If someone had to be beaten up, it was I who did the "disciplining." What these girls had sensed correctly was that I did not have the low posture and the sheepishness expected of newcomers. I did not kowtow to girls barely two years older than myself. What they could not have known was my ranking in my own family, where I was equal to my older sisters and, on occasion, took the role of their protector.

This ambush did not achieve its purpose. I methodically went after the girls who had ganged up on me and beat them up one after the other. The word got around quickly. I was never beaten up again. It also caused the "little ones" to attach themselves to me for protection year after year. It established myself as different within the narrow confines of the PL dormitory and the public schools we moved through together.

Is there a neutral area of activities that is open to individual initiative and free expression? There is in the world of arts, specifically that most superficial part of the arts concerned with aesthetics. Looks, colors, gestures, fabrics, texture, are usually sufficiently non-threatening to established cultural values and expectations, but lend themselves to endless discussions and apparent controversy. Within these limits, we were able to express our artistic talents and acting abilities. The occasion came once a month when all birthdays in that month were combined for one celebration. Each room was asked to work up a performance. That is what I remember as fun. It was self entertainment. We produced a wide variety of skits and musical numbers, for which we wrote, directed, choreographed, acted and supplied all the necessary sound and lighting, as well as costumes, sets, and makeup. And always, we competed as though the Oscars were at stake.

Winning, however, is different in Japan from winning in Western societies. In Japan, it is almost impossible to compete and win as an individual. If that happens you shine too much, you stick out too far, and the "nail that sticks out, has to be hammered down," as the old Japanese saying goes. As a group you may win. However, the process of picking the group winner is also different. All members of all groups participate in making the choice. Usually, this is done by voice or hand vote. And that means that the popularity of a competing group can be more important than the brilliance or lack thereof of their performance. If this all works well, the group spirit has been reinforced and all feel good about belonging.

There was another difference to Western societies—no audience. After weeks of intensive rehearsals, we performed solely for our own entertainment. Where, as I found out later, American parents will attend dutifully and wax ecstatic over the theatrical exertions of their kindergarten offspring, no parents or any other adults came to our performances.

4

You Are The Sunshine Of My Heart

The life I lead today started when I was fourteen years old. I was sent to join my older brother and sister in the Perfect Liberty dormitory in Tokyo. For the first time in many years, we could see each other every day, although we still lived in separate quarters and led our own lives. I entered public Junior High School in Tokyo, famous for high academic standards, athletic achievements and a fiercely competitive spirit. I thrive on competition. This was my kind of environment.

At Yoyogi Junior High School, examination results were posted by name along the walls surrounding the campus. Each time we walked by, we could either reassure ourselves of our excellence or be depressed anew. From the beginning, I ranked among the top 10% in all subjects, high enough to be admitted to advanced math courses. These courses were taught an hour before school started and girls were strongly discouraged from enrolling. In my math class there were five girls among 50 students. This was exhilarating to me, because at Perfect Liberty such "choice" did not exist. In addition to doing well academically, I competed successfully in high jump, track meet and softball. Every morning at the assembly in the schoolyard, the principal would announce the winners of the previous competitions. I heard my name called out often. Thus was my ego and self-confidence reinforced in ways rare in Japanese society. I could not and would not boast, one of the worst lapses in good manners, but I learned quietly that I would be able to take care of whatever problems might come my way.

Tokyo is divided into 23 districts. One of those, Shibuya, is where Yoyogi is located. In a country where everything is ranked in hierarchical order, Shibuya stands near the top of Tokyo neighborhoods. The fact that movie stars, high ranking American military officers, and their families lived there, was not lost on us. It only intensified the sheer excitement of being in one of the great cities of the world, where 10% of the entire Japanese population lives.

At Yoyogi Jr. High, I had my first English class. Mr. Mori, my teacher, was a young man with thick glasses, who had worked for Americans at the nearby U.S. Army base. He spoke and taught us American-English as distinct from the Japanese-

English taught by most Japanese English teachers. Japanese-English amounts to handicapping students by teaching them to pronounce words by adding a vowel to English words that end in consonants. For example, salad becomes *salada*. Virtually no Japanese English teacher could speak English fluently, but they could read and write and translate Shakespeare and other advanced texts. Their goal was to prepare us to pass the next examination. Grammar was their daily bread. Learning how to speak English was not. We went home with our grammar drill books to do extra assignments in translation of texts, which often were beyond our comprehension.

We had practiced good handwriting from our first day in school. A beautiful calligraphy was an important part of Japanese culture before typewriters and word processors "equalized" the writing skills of writers. To this day Japanese brush calligraphy, for example, impresses Westerners like art. When I learned to write, handwriting was also still considered an expression of the writer's character and degree of education. Potential employers asked that résumés be handwritten. Love letters, often the first "intimate" contact between boy and girl, were a matter of utmost concern for the writer. Where to a Western lover eye contact, facial expression and body language are important first impressions, for the Japanese suitor the all-important first impression would come from his or her handwriting.

When I was fourteen, I received such a letter from a boy in my school. Almost before I read it, I fell in love with his beautiful handwriting. When the writer mentioned that his uncle was a famous writer, whose name I recognized, I knew I was deeply in love. When I read, "you are the sunshine of my heart," probably the lyrics of some popular song, my heart melted. Our "affair" progressed in typical Japanese fashion. We would occasionally exchange furtive glances during official school events, never actually date, but continue to exchange soulful letters in beautiful handwriting. We only met twice. I arranged to see him, before I left for America. I cannot remember what was said. To be alone with a boy was so unusual that we did not know how to act. No holding of hands, no kissing, no heavy petting. Our second meeting happened years later on the Osaka subway. I was holding onto a strap in a crowded car, when the train took a turn and threw me against the person next to me. As I said "excuse me" I looked into his face and recognized my first "lover." We both blushed, like before, and it took us a moment before we could talk. I told him that I had been in America studying and was back for my first visit during summer vacation. He told me that he was working for a textile company that exported to America. The station we both got off came soon. There might have been more to say, but we parted and never saw each other again.

With English now established as the world language or *lingua franca,* all Japanese must learn the English alphabet and be able to read and write at least their names in Romanized spelling. Passports cannot have only Japanese writing. Since the 1964 Olympic Games in Tokyo most station signs, billboards, show window displays and traffic directives are printed in English. In addition, English is freely used for aesthetic purposes often with very imaginative spelling and grammar. Some of the difficulty and unintentional humor comes from the fact that in Japanese there are no "r" and "l" sounds. Where they occur in English, it is almost impossible for Japanese to be sure which one they hear, or which one to use, when speaking or writing. I have seen a mother and son walking down a street in Lake Kawaguchi, a small resort town at the foot of Mt. Fuji, both wearing identical T-shirts with vile profanity in English running down their backs. A sign over the entrance to a hair salon simply said, "Come Hair!" There are now also many "Health Crubs" and "Beauty Saloons," where one can get one's hair "brow dry" while having a "nice lest."

I was fortunate that for my early English training, Mr. Mori, who spoke normal English, corrected the typical mistakes taught by other Japanese English teachers. But to this day my mind is programmed to double check, for a fraction of a second, words with "l" and "r" before I use them. To pronounce words like "parallel" took me years to learn. At my wedding, I stumbled over the word "perplexity."

Mr. Mori invited some of the American officers' wives to our class as guest speakers. That was my first personal contact with foreigners. I not only looked forward to those visits intensely, but also became one of the few students in my class who would eagerly participate in "conversations" with the American ladies. One, Mrs. White, asked us to describe her. She was middle-aged, well dressed, with silver hair and blue eyes and a very light complexion. She reminded me of the flawlessly beautiful movie stars walking or vamping through American movies. Mrs. White was wearing a strand of pearls, probably Mikimoto pearls purchased in Japan.

"You look very nice," I said.

"Thank you," said Mrs. White, smiling with a set of beautifully straight and white teeth.

I learned two things: Americans have beautiful teeth and they know how to accept a compliment with grace and simplicity. Orthodontistry was then practically unknown in Japan as it was in the rest of the world. Straight teeth were the exception in Japan rather than the rule. To acknowledge a compliment graciously was almost totally outside Japanese culture.

If someone told my mother that she looked nice, she would cover her mouth with her hand bow her head in complete embarrassment and whisper, "Oh no! I look so terrible! Always!"

I made a mental note to say thank you when complimented by Americans. However, this did not come naturally or quickly and to this day, I cannot quite bring myself to be so demonstrative among my Japanese friends or relatives.

English became my favorite subject. I listened to the American Forces Network (AFN) and sought out every opportunity to practice what I had learned. I would walk up to *gaijin* (foreigners) who, to me, looked lost, offering directions whether they needed them or not.

One day our Mr. Mori did not show up for class. I thought he was sick, but we learned that he was killed in a train accident rumored to be a suicide.

Before transferring to High School there was an interlude during which a Mr. Dobbin taught us British English. He took a dim view of American English and corrected our "sloppy" pronunciation. His aim was to teach the Queen's English, but the Queen meant little to us. We could not hear her sing on AFN, none of her speeches from the throne were broadcast in Japan. There were no British soldiers stationed in Japan. Democracy and modernity had been brought to us by "emperor" Douglas MacArthur and it had been achieved in a largely civilized and enlightened way. If there was any foreign country that our *après guerre* generation was excited about and whose culture we were impressed by and willing to copy lock, stock and barrel, it was America.

General MacArthur had written a new Japanese Constitution that in addition to including the first ten amendment freedoms of the US Constitution gave women equal rights with men. I did not specifically know this, but I knew that women were treated better in America from my limited personal observation of American women who came to our school and from American movies, where Katherine Hepburn and Rosalind Russell and others demonstrated that women could take care of business and themselves and could, indeed, sometimes triumph over men.

My idol was Vivian Leigh's Scarlet O'Hara. In my fantasies, I could fully identify with her indomitable spirit. I, too, had overcome considerable adversity by that time. I knew that one thing that would never occur to me would be the thought of giving up. There would always be Tara. My Tara would be America. And so, the idea of going to America began to take form in my mind. I was still only 14 years old, but I knew that if I wanted to be serious about this "plan," I must do two things: learn all the English I could and not tell anyone about my plan, least of all my parents.

One of the reasons I had studied so hard in junior high school was to pass the entrance examinations to one of the best High Schools in Tokyo. However, this was not to be. Just when

I was ready, Perfect Liberty moved its headquarters to Osaka onto newly acquired, only partially developed, land. Out of the blue came the order for us to pack up and move to the new headquarters. To this day, I have not completely lived down my shock and resentment over being ordered to leave Tokyo and to give up my dream to enter High School there. But once my father had made the decision to bring his whole family into Perfect Liberty, our freedom to make choices was, for all practical purposes, over. From then on, my father was often transferred from one place to another. We were all moved by the dictates of the Holy Father and his aides. This would be my life, if I did not find a way to escape.

Meanwhile, my new address was Osaka, known to the world as a center of commerce and culture, fine cuisine and prosperity. None of this was part of our lives at Perfect Liberty. The new territory was outside the city and was as wild as anything could be wild in Japan. We lived in temporary shacks while the permanent buildings were being raised. We built them. Like Chinese coolies, we walked uphill in the mud, balancing two straw buckets full of soil at the end of wooden poles laid across our shoulders. With every step, we would sink ankle deep into the mud. Still we had to move fast to the whistle of the foreman who was also the one to refill our buckets. With short periods of rest and a lunch break, we worked until dark. Afterwards in the *ofuro,* we could hardly touch our shoulders. They were swollen and raw. It was a strenuous way to spend our summer vacation, but not a complaint was heard.

The new buildings were primitive. Each grade had one classroom. The teachers' offices were little rabbit hutches. Our library was tiny. Even our teachers were of the cut-rate kind, either extremely young and inexperienced, or old, burnt out and always ready to go to sleep. I sometimes roasted soybeans over our Bunsen burner in Chemistry class, to the snoring accompaniment of our teacher. From a very competitive and stimulating environment, I experienced a complete letdown. It became a challenge for me to keep my mind occupied beyond boring class routines that I could usually finish within minutes after they were assigned. It became my habit always to carry my own books and hide them under the class textbooks. I was frequently caught and sent to the principal's office. Instead, I would detour to the library and read some more.

From time to time, I led groups of coconspirators in circumventing some of the rules. One such was that we were not to celebrate Christmas. I liked the idea of singing Christmas songs in English. I made a small booklet of Christmas carols and practiced them with some of my friends. We had no tree and no trimmings, but when Christmas came around, we had smuggled both into our assembly hall. There were the tree cutters who brought the tree into the hall. There was the beautiful decoy girl who enticed our young dormitory master to go stargazing with her, while the tree was brought in. There were the "production line workers" who sang for and helped the makers of tree trimmings in return for getting their rejects for free. When all was in place, and with lookouts posted in strategic places, we sang our carols softly in the dark and munched goodies someone had miraculously collected. All went by without the "enforcers" noticing anything, and we were not punished.

Within three years, the new Perfect Liberty Headquarters had transformed itself from an explorer's camp into a self-contained and self-sufficient commune in which every member was assigned certain tasks and all were serviced and taken care of.

"From each according to his abilities, to each according to his needs" could have been our motto.

Not until much later, in America of all places, did I learn that this was a key concept in Marxist Communism. But for me the implications of our Perfect Liberty life style were clear. I would turn into an ant in an anthill. If I behaved safely, I need never worry again. I would be married, have children, age and die all within the security of Perfect Liberty. All I needed to give up would be my liberty, perfect or otherwise.

I redoubled my efforts to learn English. I searched out and found a pen pal in Canada. We were the same age and had surprisingly much to share and write about. One secret we shared was the number of pimples I had sprouted. *Post haste* Wilma sent me soaps and salves to help me in my hour of embarrassment. We also exchanged delicacies that neither of us had tasted before and, though our growing friendship forbade us to admit it at the time, really did not like. Thus was I introduced to licorice candy, and Wilma to rice crackers wrapped in seaweed. We continued to exchange gifts, but they had to be small. I could hardly afford the postage. Today it is a matter of amazement to me how we were able to bridge the cultural abyss. I knew near to nothing about Western culture in general and Canadian lifestyles in particular. Wilma, my pen pal with a beautiful handwriting, must have known even less about Japan. But when it comes to determination, I had met my match. Over a lifetime, we became soul mates and our correspondence never stopped.

In my second year in High School, I organized an English Speaking Society. A guest speaker was recommended to us by the local YMCA. This is how Vernon Spencer came into our lives. Mr. Spencer was an improbably handsome young American from California studying Japanese architecture in Kyoto. I would meet him at the train station and walk him back to Perfect Liberty all the while trying out my pitiful English on this most articulate and naturally charming man. Instead of correcting me all the time he laughed a lot, which I found even more charming. There was no way for me not to have a serious crush on him. When we learned that he already had a Japanese girlfriend, who later became his wife, we were united in our disappointment. However, what impressed me the most, and became the basis of our lifelong friendship, was that he treated me with respect. For the first time in my life I had met someone who took me unconditionally seriously. Mr. Spencer showed us photographs of his family. One shot showed his sister on the beach in California. The sun, the space, the beauty did it to me. That was the place I wanted to be. Would be!

Mr. Spencer was the only teacher in my experience in Japan who could get a group of Japanese students to actually speak English beyond sheer memorization. He got us involved in skits and prepared me for a speech contest, which I did not win. To be with Mr. Spencer was fun. That learning could be "fun" was an entirely new experience for all of us. He taught us to laugh with him instead of laugh at him or giggle. We could tease him and make him blush, thoughts that would never have occurred to us with our Japanese teachers. He brought genuine warmth to our meetings. That is something we were not used to. Warmth is not a huge item in Japanese culture once a child enters school. Japanese teachers and adults in general tend to think that warmth and respect are incompatible. Mr. Spencer showed to us that this need not be so. If this was how people acted in America, I would not fear living among them.

First, I had to finish High School. Our student body had increased. Our baseball team had won the national championships. That had put our school on the map and made it a popular place to apply to. We had new buildings to meet this demand. Perfect Liberty had, indeed, become one of the most prosperous new religious groups in Japan. It had acquired the nickname "golf religion," stemming from the organization's business genius of turning the flat roofs of its churches into golf courses. A separate high school had been added where the students could work as caddies during the day and study at night. From time to time even some day students, myself included, were pressed into caddy service. Golf had become a major source of income. Piety was not a requirement to play as long as you could pay.

In my second year in Perfect Liberty High School, it was the task of our counselors to steer students either into courses preparatory to entering a university or vocational subjects. The ground rule was: girls towards vocational, boys towards university. There were exceptions. Boys, who were not expected to succeed in academia, were allowed to continue with vocational training. No such reverse exceptions applied to girls. I pleaded to be allowed to take university-oriented courses, but was denied. The day of my graduation was approaching. In Japan, we did not and still do not have junior high and high school proms and parties. Students go through graduation ceremonies, which are somber affairs, because they mark the separation from peers and transition to academic or vocational training. Sad music accompanies tearful farewells as the students march out of the auditorium towards the school gates. Proud, but subdued parents applauded as we came marching down the aisle.

5

Become A Stone In America

✦

Amerika No Ishi Ni Nare

さんとす丸南米船船記念
昭和35年4月2日神戸出帆
大阪商船

My choices after graduation from Perfect Liberty High School were few and virtually all directing me towards becoming a good Japanese woman. Finishing school was the logical next step. I made one attempt at breaking away. In my school uniform, the only decent formal dress I had, I went to Osaka to apply for a job as a stewardess with Japan Air Lines. This was at the time when being a stewardess was considered glamorous. But for me it also would have meant to get away from Perfect Liberty and to make contacts with foreigners. At Japan Air Lines, I walked into a scene that could have been backstage of a fashion show. My competitors were dressed to kill and it seemed to me that I, in my Perfect Liberty school uniform, with ponytails and no makeup, was the one to be killed—easily. I had passed the English test. That had brought down the number of applicants from over 500 to less than 50, who were now assembled for personal interviews.

Clutching my letter of acceptance as a finalist, I walk into the interviewing room. The door closes behind me. I am facing eight men sitting in a half circle around a podium.

"Step up and turn around," one of them instructs me.

"Why do you want to become a stewardess?" another one wants to know.

"You know you would have to do something about your hair," one of the men volunteers.

End of questions.

From then on, their attention and interest was entirely and intensely on my appearance. I was lost, I knew it, and the men ogling me knew it. Glamour was not my thing. Grammar was.

It was back to Perfect Liberty Finishing School for girls. This is what my parents expected. Their daughter would learn to cook, sew, arrange flowers, serve tea properly, wear a formal Kimono graciously, bow well, deeply and long, smile demurely, obey the male powers that be, and never show a trace of her own will power. They would watch with pride and satisfaction, as I turned into an attractive, desirable graduate, ready for an arranged marriage. My secret plan to go to America was on hold. Finishing school, however, would provide me with a "cover." To my parents and other family members, finally all seemed well with their *yancha musume,* the worrisome tomboy in the family.

One topic not covered at that time in Japanese public schools through High School was sex education. In my coeducational Junior High School that was one day when boys and girls were separated. This is when one of our old spinster teachers came into class to instruct us about menstruation. This was early warning for us. None of us had started having periods.

Now at Perfect Liberty Finishing School where the personal life style of the Perfect Liberty leaders was thoroughly modern and enlightened in that it allowed, as a matter of course, affairs and "second" families of the male leaders, it was felt that some knowledge about sex should be part of the curriculum.

And so it came to pass that one day Dr. Katsura, a dentist, was asked to come to our class to start our sex education. He was a good looking, thirty-something, married man with children. The day he was scheduled to talk to us, no one cut class. The room was filled with anticipation and excitement. Finally, the great taboo would be broken, the mysteries and, more importantly, the mechanics of love revealed.

"Sex," Dr. Katsuro began with intense embarrassment, "happens on your wedding night. That is when the man's penis will swell up and become big. The man will then know what to do with it and you just lie there and do nothing. Don't fight! Don't refuse! By all means, don't scream! It might hurt in the beginning, because you are tense, but it will get better."

Dr. Katsura concluded, "Sex is a little like picking your nose. Any questions?"

Not one hand went up. But as the sexpert turned his back, we all broke into uncontrollable laughter.

The plan at Perfect Liberty was to induct as many girls as possible graduating from finishing school, into training towards becoming Divine Sisters or be placed in arranged marriages. I opted for the former and returned to Tokyo. I lived at the Tokyo branch of Perfect Liberty, while I studied English at the Meguro Interpreter School purportedly in preparation to my going abroad to spread the word of Perfect Liberty. I shared a room with Piiko-san, one of the Holy Father's brother's mistresses, who enjoyed certain special privileges like having her own clothes tailor made, when the rest of us were still wearing only Perfect Liberty uniforms. Through my close association with Piiko-san, I gained insights into the inner workings of Perfect Liberty. Simply put, it was not different from other established major religions. There was a thoroughly corrupt upper echelon of "holy" men, all living with multiple "divine" sisters who might carry titles such as secretaries or adopted daughters. Cadillac limousines, first-class journeys around the world, studies abroad for some of the "close contacts" were common.

I learned much about the widespread corruption in an organization based on high moral concepts, if not the one God concept dominant in Christianity and Islam. But I also learned the age-old truth that privilege, wealth, and the freedoms they can afford do not necessarily add up to happiness. At Perfect Liberty the intrigues and backstabbing, jealousies and pettiness reminded me of what I had learned about the inner workings of former Samurai dynasties. Now they played as superficially and false as modern soap operas.

When English speaking guests came to Perfect Liberty, I was called upon to translate, show them around and take care of their needs. Never did I let an opportunity go by without asking the guests if they could find me a sponsor in America. One day Mr. and Mrs. Grubb arrived from California. I made my usual appeal as we walked the now immaculately kept grounds of the Perfect Liberty compound, replete with golf courses and ponds stocked with expensive, colorful *koi* fish. They said they would look for someone when they returned home. I began to correspond with them to remind them of their promise. One day I received the letter I had been waiting for. The Grubbs informed me that they had found an American childless couple willing to sponsor and pay for my one-way passage to America. I was to care for a handicapped wife while going to college. The sponsors they had found were Mr. and Mrs. Lloyd Wilson. They sent me an affidavit of support and a check for a one-way passage by steamer. I responded with due speed, got a passport and visa, changed Yen into the $50 maximum then allowed to be taken out of the country by Japanese citizens, and purchased a third-class steamship ticket. When I had everything in order and the departure date of my ship was only one week away, I called my parents.

"I am going to America," I said in my best Finishing School manner.

There was a moment of silence at the other end, and then I heard my father repeating what I had said and my stepmother screaming, "Do something to stop her!"

Later, on my pre-departure visit home, I explained, "I am going to America to spread the word for Perfect Liberty and to study English for six months."

Although my father sensed that this was not true, the two of us went through an elaborate ritual to make it seem that way.

For example, my father watching me pack would then retrieve certain items from my luggage announcing loudly, "That you don't need, you'll be gone for only half a year!"

He and I conspired in this pretense for different reasons. The family needed to believe that I was merely going to America for a visit. Thus, my mother's plans for an arranged marriage would only be postponed. My training in Finishing School would not have been in vain. The combined expectations of other family members and friends would not be dashed.

For my father, then a high functionary in Perfect Liberty, it was even more important to maintain the fiction of a limited visit abroad to calm considerable opposition to my leaving among other Perfect Liberty members.

At one meeting some of my fellow sisters had angrily asked the Holy Father, "Why should one so lowly in the organization be allowed such a privilege?"

Mean rumors were spread about me and shared in letters to my family. One of the most ludicrous was that I had stolen food from the kitchen and given it to the baseball players. The Holy Father rose to the challenge explaining that my leaving was not his but only my doing.

To make it all somewhat more palatable, he added, "In America Sister Tanegashim will be working as a maid while spreading the word for Perfect Liberty."

No one could object to that. In fact, I would be the first one to do so and become everyone else's role model. This subterfuge continued for a few years. I did, indeed, visit and stay in loose touch with a very small first overseas branch of Perfect Liberty in Los Angeles. But later, when Perfect Liberty Headquarters sent me a large package of twenty-dollar raffle tickets for me to sell, I sent it all back.

On the day of my departure, my family and a group of my friends came to Kobe harbor to send me off. My father asked the captain of the *Santos-Maru,* a ship taking Japanese immigrants to Brazil, to take good care of me. Gongs sounded and sad music warned visitors to go ashore. Everybody cried and I started to cry, too.

As my father turned to go he whispered, "Be a stone in America!"

I knew what he meant. I would live and die there. He knew that I was leaving Japan for good.

"We may not see her again," he told my mother. "Don't make a fuss and spoil our last moments together."

 I was standing on deck as our ship was slowly towed out of Kobe harbor holding on to one end of my roll of colorful tape, which my father was unraveling on shore. The moment came when everyone's tape roll had reached its end. I turned around towards my new life. It was April 2, 1960.

Standing there was another girl my age, who had watched my leave taking. She had gone through the same scene earlier in Yokohama.

"Foreign student?" she asked.

"Yes," I replied.

"Me too. I'm Ayako, what's your name?"

"Kaori. I'm going to Los Angeles."

"Ah so!" she said, "I'm going to Kansas."

"Let's meet later after I've found my cabin."

I descended into the lower bowels of the ship and found my cabin. There were six bunk beds separated by curtains. Just like in the Perfect Liberty dormitories. As I settled in, the door opened and in walked Ayako. Our bunks were next to each other. We did not know it then, but this would be the beginning of a lifelong friendship. It started with both of us being violently seasick. The thought of eating made us feel worse.

Moreover, even had we wanted to eat, it would have been a difficult task. The ship was rocking so badly that the food served in the steerage mess hall flew back and forth from one end to the other. The floor drenched in *miso* soup. We supported each other up the ladders to the deck and retched into the sea. Eventually the sea calmed and so did our stomachs. With our sea sickness over we were instantly back to full health and ready to explore our new world.

A quick inventory of our "assets" revealed that we had certain things in common. We both had sung in choruses. She sang alto and I sang soprano. We knew, and had practiced, the same songs. As we sang, we could spontaneously harmonize. We were the same age. It was clear to me that my new friend had exceptional beauty. She was also very proper in the Japanese fashion, but, fortunately, upon my prodding, opened up to enter the social whirl that takes hold of a passenger liner as soon as it leaves harbor.

I played my "connections." Only hours after our recovery, we received several invitations for dinner, parties and games. The captain whom my father had talked to, saw to it that we ate and spent most of our time upstairs in First Class, where the food and accommodations and service were decidedly nicer than in the bottom with its flying rice bowls and splashing *miso* soup and army cots stacked on top of each other.

We became the mascots of the ship's officers and crew. We could go where we pleased. Everyone knew and welcomed us. Our passage to America turned into two charmed weeks. We were happy and made those around us happy. We were vibrant, outgoing and innocent. Innocence was our shield and all our many gentlemen suitors accepted it in good grace. The age of casual intimate relationships might have been upon us. However, on our voyage it was not so.

I was keeping a diary and noticed that April 7, my birthday, came twice. The purser explained that we had just crossed the international dateline. This was the only time in my life that I celebrated my birthday two days in a row, a fitting way to pass from my teens into my 20's. The night before our arrival in Los Angeles, still on the high seas, Ayako and I made our debut as a singing duo at the ship's talent show. In our category, we won first prize. There were, apparently, no Hollywood talent agents in the audience. No irresistible offers came our way, but we got a taste of the high that comes with a standing ovation.

Our ship pulled into Los Angeles harbor in midmorning. I had been unable to eat breakfast. I kept looking at the photograph Mr. Wilson had exchanged for mine. As we docked, I searched the faces of the welcoming crowd. No Mr. Wilson. Already I saw myself standing at the pier, all the other passengers gone, only I alone forgotten with my two suitcases. Then I saw Mr. Grubb who had come to pick me up in his grandiose Cadillac to deliver me to my new home. My two suitcases disappeared into the huge trunk, big enough, I thought, to house a Japanese family of four. Soon we were on the freeway moving with the flow of traffic. I did not see a tollbooth at the freeway entrance. That, I thought, must be why they called them "free ways." There is no such thing in Japan. Even for short distances on the super highways, stiff tolls are collected.

I seemed to be drifting in a sea of wealth. Large American cars all around me. One person in each car. So many lanes! So much space! So much sky! So much sun! A city so casually spreading towards the horizon. Few high rises. An endless expanse of single homes. Was everybody rich in America? Was the America of the movies I had seen reality after all? Would this be my new life now?

6

Where's The Cole Slaw?

Mr. Grubb pulled up at my sponsor's house in Montebello. I carried my belongings into an average tract home in an average neighborhood of which I learned there were thousands in the Los Angeles Basin. The front door let us directly into the living room. There sat Mrs. Wilson, looking in my direction through prescription glasses, smiling. Mr. Grubb had already explained to me that she had "tunnel vision." I tried looking through my closed fist to see what that would be like. She could see very little, I realized, and needed help. It was a brain tumor, she later explained to me, that had brought on this condition.

"Would you like something to eat, something to drink?" asked Mrs. Wilson.

"Oh no, please no!" I said.

I was, in fact, very hungry, but on my best Japanese behavior, I could not accept after being asked only once. In Japan, I would now be served anyway, and I expected this to happen here, too. Instead, Mrs. Wilson went on to other things and food dropped from our conversation. As my stomach growled, I made a mental note never to let Japanese modesty get in the way of getting food in America.

This first lesson I not only learned quickly, but also too well. Within a very short time after my arrival in the land of milk and honey, butter and mayonnaise, potato and gravy, all foods I had never had in quantities in Japan, I had gained twenty-five pounds. I could no longer laugh or sit down without zippers and buttons popping. The sack dress then in fashion saved me. It was a relief to find out that my beautiful and slim shipboard friend Ayako was going through the same kind of growth in Kansas, where she was corn and potato fed. When we exchanged pictures, we laughed away our difficulties in recognizing the old "us." Already on the ship, I had begun to sample Western food in ways and quantities like never before. But my full-scale introduction to a daily Western diet came the morning after I arrived in the Wilson household. In my application, I had mentioned that I could cook. A minor overstatement.

"You know how to cook scrambled eggs, don't you?" Mrs. Wilson said before I went to sleep.

"Yes," I replied and then went to look up the word "scrambled" in my English-Japanese dictionary. Looking under "skla...."

To scramble eggs in Japan we use chopsticks to "beat" the eggs and then cut them into little pieces as they fry. Another way is to let the beaten eggs set in the pan, and then slice it into strips or squares. To both sugar is usually added.

I served my first breakfast with some trepidation but hoping, frankly, to be complimented. Looking without looking, I watched Mr. Wilson take his first bite.

"What did you put into this?" he asked as he spit out the egg.

"Sugar," I replied eyes downcast

"I never heard of such a thing!" said Mr. and Mrs. Wilson in unison shaking their heads as though they had rehearsed their reply together.

Sandwich lunch passed without incident. But my career as an American cook got worse before it got better. Mrs. Wilson and I discussed dinner and she decided that a chicken noodle casserole with coleslaw would be a good idea.

"Do you know how to prepare this?" she asked.

"Yes."

It was back to the dictionary. "K A S E L O"? That is what I heard clearly. There was nothing like it in my dictionary. I had to ask Mrs. Wilson for the spelling. Then came "co-slow." No problem—slow cooking together.

"Here are the ingredients," said Mrs. Wilson. "Boil water and put the noodles in until they are done, then strain them on a colander. Scrape the meat off the chicken bones. Slice the cabbage. Put it all into the casserole dish."

I cooked noodles and looked for a "calendar," as I thought she had said. There was a big one hanging on the kitchen wall.

As I lined up the noodles in neat rows on the calendar sheet I thought, "What a strange way Americans have to dry their noodles."

I mixed it all together and cooked it slowly. The final product looked great to me and, again, I served it with hope.

"Where's the coleslaw?" asked Mrs. Wilson

"It's in the casserole," I replied.

That was another thing the Wilson's had never heard of in their lives. I adapted quickly to cooking homemade fast food dishes. Hamburgers, fried chicken and hot dogs became my staples. Japanese rice and pickled vegetables, dried fish and *miso* soup, seaweed, raw fish and roe were memories of times gone by. Japanese food had not become popular in America, as yet. Supermarkets did not carry it. The few Japanese restaurants then in existence had exotic appeal to a rich gourmet clientele. I was neither rich nor could I imagine eating Japanese food as being exotic. The Japanese diet consists of mostly fish and vegetables. This begins with breakfast, which is usually tofu in *miso* soup. *Miso* is a multipurpose soybean paste and is used as a protein base or supplement in many dishes. Other breakfast items include dried fish, seaweed, pickled vegetables, and an occasional raw egg. There may be *natto*. These are fermented soybeans. The gooey, stringy dark brown mass looks like peanut butter, but has a taste and smell of rotten food. It is an acquired taste most Westerners do not easily acquire. Of course, there is always rice and tea. A Japanese lunch, the light meal of the day, may be noodle soup with a variety of vegetables and processed fish cakes in bright colors to enhance the aesthetics of the dish. Lunch can also be Chinese food like dumplings, fried noodles and fried rice. Two "foreign" lunch items in wide distribution are curried rice and spaghetti with catsup. They are offered in identical quantities and taste at most Japanese railroad stations.

Japanese dinner is the most elaborate meal of the day. In a typical Japanese inn, two dozen little dishes may be set out for the traveler returning to his room after *ofuro*. Included may be shrimp, fresh fish, pork, chicken and, rarely, very little beef sliced wafer thin. This is accompanied by vegetables in season, bamboo shoots in the spring, *matsutake* mushrooms in the fall. Food in Japan is generally expensive. Many items are bought and served only for special occasions throughout the year. Portions served in restaurants and at home are small by American standards. Japanese are trained from childhood on to eat with their eyes. Exceptional care goes into the preparation, decoration and serving of meals. Often what arrives in front of the diner looks more like a piece of art than mere food.

Fruit in Japan are luxury items. If their vitamin intake depended on it, most Japanese would die of scurvy early. Today I know that most human beings stick to the basic foods they were raised with from babyhood on. Germans tell me that they cannot be too long without dark, heavy bread and potatoes. The French must have food smothered in their famous sauces mopped up to the last drop with pieces torn from mile long baguettes. Italians are desolate without spaghetti three times a day. Danes judge a day a failure if it did not start with half a dozen different cheeses. I began to have a craving for Japanese rice. It differs from American rice, which is judged ideal when it is dry and fluffy. Japanese rice is sticky, but not soggy. This is the right consistency for chopsticks to pick up. It is also simply the consistency that Japanese are used to. We judge the quality of Sushi, for example, by the rice it comes with and the freshness of the other ingredients. The type of rice and how it is cooked becomes more important than caviar or other vastly more expensive accompaniments.

I could not find my rice in our neighborhood markets. However, looking for it led me to discover other Japanese living in the Los Angeles area. I found that there was, in fact, a type of networking among them that would eventually be of immense help to me emotionally, socially and professionally. I discovered Little Tokyo. I learned that this section of downtown Los Angeles had been in existence for a long time as a center of culture and commerce, dominated by flower and produce markets supplied by Japanese tenant farmers. These *Issei*, first generation Japanese immigrants, pioneered the growing of Japanese rice in

America. It was all interrupted by their removal to concentration camps during World War II for "their own safety," as they were told.

Upon their return after the war, Little Tokyo was rebuilt. When I first saw it, it was a thriving community with four Buddhist Temples, hundreds of stores, eating and drinking places, senior housing and cheap lodging for laborers. Later a major cultural center with a theater and museum, upscale hotels and retirement homes were added. This is where I found the rice I craved. This is where I could speak my language and behave like a Japanese. For an hour or so, I did not have to be constantly on guard.

I began to make new friends in America. One of the first was a Japanese woman, who had arrived here fifteen years before me as a war bride. Now she was part of a welcoming committee that tried to ease newcomers from Japan into the community. When she first invited me to her house, I was not only looking forward to meeting new friends, but also to a genuine Japanese Sushi meal. The table was set. Everything looked perfectly Japanese. I bite into a piece of *makizushi* (rolled shushi) and am shocked. Normally, ingredients are cucumbers, eggs, spinach, *kampyoo* inside of a gourd, raw fish and roe rolled into sushi rice and seaweed. Here now, the cucumbers were sticks of celery, eggs were *takuwan*, yellow pickled radish. The raw fish was ham and cheese. This was my introduction to Yankee culinary ingenuity. I knew enough of Japanese manners to compliment my hostess profusely. Today, of course, Japanese cuisine in America has become popular partly because it has adapted to Western taste and brought forth such things as California Roll, which was unknown in Japan before and is resented by the traditionally trained Sushi makers.

"We don't even have avocado," one of them hissed at me when I tried to order California roll to introduce an American friend to Sushi the easy way.

Meanwhile, there was a change in the Wilson household. Mrs. Wilson was going to be in Oakland for an advanced training for the blind. Propriety demanded that I not stay in the house with her husband alone during her absence. This was the beginning of my foster homes period. The Grubbs, who had welcomed me to America, became my first substitute parents. By then Mrs. Grubb was working towards a master's degree in psychology. I became her maid and in-house subject for psychoanalytical experimentations. Our daily routine started with the bath. Mrs. Grubb, whom her friends called Tiny, was indeed small of stature and she reminded me often that she had once done nude modeling. She liked to have her back scrubbed while she soaked in the tub. Between rubbing and complimenting her, I rushed to prepare breakfast and pack a lunch for Mr. Grubb to take to his constructions work. Before Mrs. Grubb left for school, she would hand me a long list of things to do, enough to leave me exhausted by the time the Grubbs returned home at the end of the day.

"What else did you do today?" Mrs. Grubb would say after checking the day's list.

"Nothing."

"Well, I thought you Japanese were all so industrious?"

One night when I had prepared a steak dinner, Mrs. Grubb said, "You know Kaori, *papa-san* works really hard to feed you. Steak costs a lot of money."

I got up and went to my room to cry. Mrs. Grubb followed me.

"You are ungrateful. You are crying to get our sympathy. You are trying to escape reality by fleeing the scene. You are acting like a five-year-old child."

Living in constant analysis drove me to the edge of a nervous breakdown. I jumped if the phone or doorbell rang. I dreaded our evening meals together. I became withdrawn and depressed. That much the future psychologist was able to diagnose. After some more analysis that led nowhere, she decided I would be better off with a Japanese-American family and introduced me to the Munekiyos who became my next hosts.

They were a Nisei couple with two children, a boy and girl. Jean was college age. Wayne was still in high school and going through an awkward stage. He was uncommunicative and hardly spoke a word to me. Mr. Munekiyo was a gardener, though his own garden was tended by Helen, his wife and myself. Helen had hoped that having me around in their house would be good for her children. They might pick up some Japanese language and culture. None of the Munekiyos spoke standard Japanese, though Helen could talk to her mother in a Shimabara dialect, which I did not understand. I cooked some Japanese meals and helped with the housework. We lived in a small, neatly kept, house in Montebello, where I shared a room with daughter Jean. We took a summer school course in American history together at East Los Angeles College (ELAC) where the idea was for her to help me with an unfamiliar subject.

At our first in-class test I heard Jean whisper, "HELP!"

When I ignored her plea and got a better grade, Jean joined her brother in cutting me off. Helen's husband, Mas, was not a talkative person either.

However, one evening at dinner he said, "I am never comfortable with *hakujin*, white people."

"Why is that?" I asked.

"Haven't you ever heard that we Japanese-Americans up and down the West Coast were rounded up and moved to camps during World War II?"

"What kind of camps were those?"

"You could call them concentration camps. There were barbed wire fences and sentry towers with armed guards."

"Really?"

"We lost everything—house and belongings. Our bank accounts were frozen."

"Why? You were born and raised here, were you not?"

"Yes, we were citizens then. We still are. It didn't mean anything then."

"What about your American neighbors? Did anyone help you?"

"Help us? White people came to pick up our belongings like it was flea market day."

"How terrible!"

I learned that both Munekiyos had been part of the 120,000 Japanese-Americans living mostly on the West Coast who were removed from their homes to concentration camps for the duration of World War II. This treatment of the Japanese American population in America during the war had never been mentioned in my history classes in Japan nor in my summer school American History class.

I personally had never had cause to feel uncomfortable with or around Caucasian people. In terms of human relations in general and race relations in particular, this was an experience that raised more questions in my mind than the Munekiyos were willing to answer. Later, I talked to and read about survivors of the camps and the whole subject became an important part of my Asian-American Studies courses.

My stay with the Munekiyos was intended to be short and came to an end after only two weeks. However, this short interlude was crucial for another reason. Helen introduced me to her heavily Japanese Montebello Congregational Church. There I got my first job teaching Japanese to Sansei children on Saturdays for fifty dollars a month.

One of my classmates in the summer school class I already mentioned was an all-American girl, Nancy, who was living rent-free with the Sullivan family in exchange for light housework. When I mentioned that I needed a place to stay, she introduced me to the Sullivans to take over her job at the end of the semester. Mr. Sullivan taught English at ELAC and his wife taught the same subject at Pasadena City College. They had two children. Katie was seven, her brother Dana was five years old. As soon as I moved in, it became clear to me that the light housekeeping meant running the household and included full-time babysitting as well.

Mrs. Sullivan had a number of time-consuming serious hobbies such as playing the French horn, skiing, and more that kept her away from home a good deal of the time. Mr. Sullivan was working for his Ph.D. and did not want to be disturbed. One thing that was simple in this household was the meals. Mrs. Sullivan did not want me to get fancy. Plain hamburgers for dinner and unadorned bologna sandwiches for lunch every day. Once I tried my luck with making Chinese dumplings. The children and husband loved them.

"Mama, Kaori cooked dumplings. They tasted great!" Dana reported.

"No more of this nonsense!" retorted his mother.

I cooked spaghetti when the mother was away. I told Dana to keep it a secret, but Katie reported my transgression and I was reprimanded. Mrs. Sullivan had a way of talking like a machine gun. Hovering over me, she would fire off her criticisms like bullets. My defense was to clam up and busy myself scrubbing the oven.

"Don't shut up. Speak to me!" she would scream, as I retreated to my room.

The children, especially little Dana, began to take sides.

"Do you love Mammy?" Mrs. Sullivan would ask.

"Yes, mother. Now, can I play with Kaori?"

"Let me tie your shoe laces."

"I want Kaori to do it."

If Dana was spanked with a hairbrush or ruler for not doing his assigned chores, he would come running into my room and we would hug and cry together. At bedtime, I used to tell the boy Japanese children's stories. Peach Boy was his favorite. I had to invent different versions each night.

I was to have weekends off. But I had no money, no car, no place to go. I stayed home sewing my clothes, a skill that Mrs.

Sullivan found surprising. A pile of jeans with broken zippers was my reward. Babysitting for the weekend was quickly taken for granted.

The children and I played Japanese games together. The word got around that this Japanese girl was telling strangely exciting folk tales, and the parents of the neighborhood started bringing their children. The thought of paying me did not occur to any of them.

A Japanese game that involved creative gestures proved to be my undoing. It was years before I began teaching Asian Studies, where gestures in different cultures would be one of my favorite and most popular subjects. Now, not knowing that some of the signs we were using in our little game that had us rolling on the floor laughing, were "dirty," I scandalized the good parents when they came to pick up their kids who were working over-time with their middle fingers or thumbed their noses at each other.

My sewing attracted the attention of one of my home economics teachers, Mrs. Deneen, at ELAC. One day she complimented me in front of the class. I started crying.

"Come into my office. We'll talk." When she had closed the door behind her, she asked, "Are you having problems?"

I shook my head but couldn't stop sobbing.

"Where do you live?"

"I'm staying at the Sullivans."

"You mean Sullivan the English teacher here at the college?"

"Yes."

"Are you unhappy at the Sullivans?"

"Yes."

"Then you have to move out."

"But I have no place to go."

"I'll find one for you."

Mrs. Deneen picked up the phone and started dialing

I heard her say, "Mrs. Donovan, I have a student who needs a room. Do you have one for rent?"

She turned and asked me, "How much can you pay?"

"Fifty dollars."

"That will do. All set. You can move in any time."

Mrs. Donovan was also a home economics teacher who had recently been widowed. She lived alone in a house with three small bedrooms of which she rented out two on each side of the house. Our arrangement was that I would clean the kitchen in return for kitchen privileges. In case of emergency, I was to drive her to the hospital.

When I told the Sullivan's that I was moving out by the end of the month, Dana cried and asked, "Why do you have to leave us?"

When the time came for me to go, we both cried. But although we parted amicably, we lost touch quickly and completely.

7

You Are Not College Material

Before entering college I enrolled in adult education English and Math classes at Montebello High School, where my sponsor, Mr. Wilson, taught Mathematics. My fellow students were mostly former high school dropouts who had changed their minds and were now working towards their diplomas. One thing I learned here was to write essay exams. This had not been part of my schooling in Japan. Essay exams meant thinking on my own instead of regurgitating memorized facts. Thinking is something Japanese teachers do not encourage. For the first time I also experienced open class discussions and witnessed the spectacle of students freely asking questions and commenting on their teachers' statements. In Japan, this would be taken as defying authority. Teachers cannot deal with it. Punishment would be swift. I knew from personal experience that "correcting" my Japanese English teacher in Japan, for example, would bring immediate dismissal from the class and an "interrogation" by the principal, where the possible reasons for my insubordination would be painfully explored. Ironically, when I was now allowed to speak up and was, in fact, asked to do so, I felt constrained and awkward. By the fall of my first year in America, I became a full-time foreign student at ELAC. But first, there was an interview with the dean of admissions to determine if my English was good enough to cope with regular course work. On my appointed day, I came before Dean Herzog, an economist of German extraction.

Towering behind his desk like a grizzly bear, Mr. Herzog reached behind him, pulled a thick economics textbook from his shelf, opened it in the middle and said, "Read this chapter and tell me what it says!"

I froze. I tried to stumble through paragraphs full of terms I had never heard of. I shook my head and started crying.

"Obviously you are not college material," said Mr. Herzog, as he put his tome back onto the shelf.

Speechless, I got up and walked out. Up to this confrontation, my self-confidence was strong and securely based in my excellent scholastic record. This was my first experience with Western bluntness in a most negative fashion. In Japan, such a catastrophic putdown is possible, of course, but it will always be couched in polite language and camouflaged in smiles. The victim bows and takes all the blame as though grateful to receive it. Lives may be ruined, face may be lost, the family disgraced, but it is all done with subtlety and flawless manners in an indirect way. This had rarely been my personal experience in Japan, but it was the only model I had to deal with rejection. My next stop was with a counselor. This woman was more friendly.

"Oh, you're from Japan," she said smiling and I could see her stereotypes falling into place. "The best thing for you to take," she sang out, "would be typing and sewing."

Home Economics was the major she wrote down for me. That would make me into a good housewife. Not again! Why had I left finishing school in Osaka? But I stuck with it and got my Associate of Arts degree. It was also the last time I saw a counselor. From now on, I studied the catalogue and made up my own program. At the end of the first semester, my name went onto the Dean's List and I received a scholarship. I was hoping that Dean Herzog would take notice. However, whether he did or not, I now knew that I was, indeed, college material and his prejudices were no longer of interest to me. Only once did I meet him again. Friends had asked me to come with them on a weekend trip to Tijuana. I needed his permission to leave the country.

"Oh no," he said. "You can't do that. They'll sell you for a slave!"

Permission denied. There were, of course, the trials and tribulations of the English language. In Japan, with many compliments about my English behind me, I had fancied myself being fairly fluent. Submersion in my second language and Western culture, proved to be more of a shock and challenge than I could have expected. I should perhaps explain how much more difficult it is to come to America from a country like Japan rather than one of the European nations. Most European languages have the same roots as English. None of the Asian languages do. This creates an insecurity that is difficult to overcome. When a German says "*wasser*" instead of water, he can still be understood and, more importantly, he can still know that he is nearly correct. There is no such reassurance from Japanese to English or vice versa. The possibility of saying something dreadfully wrong is always there, because sheer memory is all you can rely on. There is no similarity in grammar or vocabulary. There are more serious differences between Asian and Western cultures, adding to the language insecurities. I cannot say that I was in a constant state of panic. However, it was not all serious all the time either. There was, for example, the time I went shopping at a hardware store.

"I need a screw," I said to the clerk.

"Yeah, sure," he said breaking into a grin. Then he shouted across the store, "Hey, Jack, this here young lady needs a screw!"

This brought down the house. I had my first taste of being a standup comedian without ever having heard of such a thing. It took me years to learn the commonly used words with sexual double meanings. Later, on my first visit to Las Vegas, where sexual innuendo is the common currency of standup comedy, I was often late in getting the point and trailing the general laughter. Much later, when I took a group of Japanese business-men as their interpreter, I had progressed to the point where I could laugh at the right moment. But my charges had no clue. By the time my translated punch line had made its way to the last one and their laughter had percolated down the line, the comedian was well into his next sketch.

"Why are you guys laughing at the wrong time?" he wanted to know.

Another semantic and very practical difficulty for Japanese visitors in America is finding the right toilet. In Japan, in my youth, it was common to find what today would be called uni-sex toilets in pubic places marked either "toilet" or "W.C." When they were separated, the signs said "gentlemen" or "ladies." Now the international logos showing a male or female figure are common. The same holds true for America, but in many places, imaginative, humorous or fancy names are used for "bathrooms," a designation for toilets only used in America, a reminder of the country's Puritan past. Not long after I arrived in America, my friend Ayako and I were invited out to a Scottish restaurant. When we looked for where to powder our noses, another American euphemism, we were confronted with "Laddies" and "Lassies." Laddies, I reasoned, must be the Scot-tish way of pronouncing ladies.

"How smart of you to figure this out," said Ayako as we walked in.

Inside we noticed a row of strange receptacles along one wall.

"This must be for spitting," I said, and we spat in unison each into our own spittoon. To our amazement, none of the stalls had doors. While Ayako used one, I stood guard in front. Suddenly the door flew open and a man rushes in with his hand on his zipper.

"Oh my God, how rude!" we screamed in unison.

The intruder froze, turned and rushed back out before we could say another word. We later learned that he did not stop, but ran right out to his car and roared off. Neither Ayako nor I could remember ever having made such a deep impression on any man. On another occasion, years later, it was my mother, here on a visit with my father, who shocked a group of urinating men in a men's room at Disneyland. My father, who had in typical Japanese fashion never moved a finger for his own care and comfort, was then dependent on my mother to take him to the toilet and hold his penis while he relieved himself. This time, my sister and I were hiding behind a tree, pretending not to belong to this couple.

No sooner had my mother and father disappeared into the men's room than the other men came running out as though they had seen Satan.

"Have you ever seen anything like this?"

The bane of a foreigner's life is the prepositions and idiomatic expressions that are so hard to look up in dictionaries.

For me it all started when a neighborhood child asked me, "How come you came to America?"

I said, "By ship."

When I was asked, "What's up," I looked up to see what might be there.

Likewise, with expressions such as "Watch out!" which made me want to go outside and look.

If I was asked "What's cooking?" I launched into an explanation of what I was making for dinner.

Being with other Japanese, their language and culture, was relaxing in a way I would never have thought possible before I left Japan. I became more aware of the Japanese networking system in the Los Angeles area and began to cultivate what in Japan we call *kone,* an example of how the Japanese shorten certain English words, in this case "connections." My enthusiasm for America grew, but I was nurturing my Japanese heritage at the same time.

There was, however, also a culture shock of a very personal kind that I could not have explained to my American sponsors and friends because they would not have understood what I was talking about. Up to my coming to America the concept of *puraibashii*—privacy—was little more to me than a foreign word. In Japan there was no space I could call my own. This was so literally as well as spiritually. Homes and apartments are generally very small. It is rare for a child to have his or her own room. Even if this were the case, parents feel free to come in at any time. Knocking is not usually part of etiquette. Often there are no doors in the Western sense of the word. Partitions may be no more than paper screens or pieces of cloth, called *noren,* hung in doorways. Walls between houses are thin and you can overhear the conversations of the neighbors. We deal with this by speaking in a low voice or whispers.

In China, people deal with this problem in the opposite way. Everyone talks loudly creating a cacophony of competing voices in which individual speech cannot be understood by those farther away.

Now in my new American home I had my own room with a solid door that I could close and lock. My own four walls. My own bed. My own window to look out of. My own air to breathe. Only myself to look at in the mirror. I walked around my room in my underwear to show myself that no one was watching me. No one was. It was exhilarating. I was high on privacy. Then I crashed. Something was wrong. I was ALONE. Why was there no one coming in, no one to meddle in my life, no one to share my space, read my letters? I had the same feeling I had had when my mother died. I felt abandoned. I had been raised to be alert and constantly respond to signals and demands coming from people around me. I had never been completely alone. To sit in my room with no other company than myself was a new and unsettling experience.

My sponsors must have sensed some of this. Their first present was a kitten. In Japan, we had tried unsuccessfully to have pets in our dormitories against the rules of the school. Now I had a pet all to myself. I named the black and white little cat "Pepe" and we became close friends. Pepe would roll himself around my neck and purr his heart out. He must have thought of himself more like a dog, because he played like a dog running after a prune pit and fetching it dutifully. His bravura number came when he tried to catch all the pop corn popping from the popper without a lid. We had a great love affair as long as it lasted until a neighbor ran him over. I would not have another pet for a very long time.

Meanwhile, ELAC was a good place for me to be a student. I joined the International Club and became its president. The high point of my presidency came when our club hosted consul generals from 17 different nations. I sat with Japan's representative and his wife at the head table. The flags of the countries were arranged around the auditorium and we all wore native costumes. For the first time in America, I wore the Kimono my mother had given me before I left Japan. Our music teacher played all the national anthems as each consul was introduced. When the singing started with the *Kimigayo*, the Japanese anthem, we all rose to sing along. I had, of course, sung and heard my anthem many times in Japan. It had never affected me emotionally. For years, I had only thoughts of leaving Japan. Here, at East Los Angeles College, I felt a lump in my throat and tears came to my eyes. This emotional rush was unexpected. It was the beginning of one more rediscovery of myself. My roots in Japanese culture and language were deep. This was something I could not change.

I had to find a way to turn this to my advantage rather than to seek to "overcome." The idea that my knowledge of Asian cultures and Japanese language might become my way to earn a living began to form in my mind. I teamed up with another foreigner, Ilca Hohn, from Germany, who was the student body president. Ilca became my inspiration, model, and closest friend. I admired her independence of spirit paired with great intelligence and beauty. I also thought she was so much luckier than I. She was fluent in English. Everyone from the college president on down liked her. This included my nemesis, Dean Herzog, who took her under his wings, making sure she received scholarships and made a smooth transition to UCLA. Try as I might, I could not be as widely popular, but I took more than a hint from her in that department, also. One such quality that I admired in Ilca was the natural straightforwardness with which she impressed people whom she met for the first time. This is definitely not the Japanese way. I knew I could not be like her, but I began to try to bring out the extrovert within me more than I had before.

Among my basic course requirements was a second foreign language. I asked to take the qualifying exam in Japanese and was told that it did not qualify anywhere in American academia as a second language. I said then I would take the test in English, which is, in fact my second language. That was an idea unheard of by the powers that determine the requirements. I took Spanish, which meant working with two dictionaries, Spanish-English and Japanese-English.

It was a challenge, but I got good grades and learned to actually converse in Spanish, though not necessarily on philosophical topics. Rather, my more down-to-earth Spanish served me well a few years later, when on a journey through Spain other passengers had taken our reserved seats on the train. When they gave no sign of moving, I threatened them with *la policía*.

I was disappointed when I learned the true meaning of *cucaracha*. In its Japanese version, the lowly cockroach had been transformed into an ode to this lovely girl named *kukaracha*. Other surprises involved *tako*—octopus—some difference from the staple at Taco Bell. Eventually, my Latino students in my language classes would come to appreciate a Japanese teacher who could, on occasion, lapse into modest Spanish.

ELAC had a number of excellent teachers. Alice Bergel, a holocaust survivor, who taught philosophy and German language, stands out in my mind. She taught me to reason rationally. She also made me see that intellectual pursuits *per se* have importance and meaning beyond their possible practical application. I had seen Kurosawa's movie *Rashomon*, for example, before I met Professor Bergel. I thought it was an interesting and captivating movie with lots of action. Bergel used the movie to explore the concept of truth. I watched the movie several times afterwards. Every time I saw it differently discovering new layers of philosophical meaning, symbolisms and intellectual possibilities.

When I graduated from ELAC with honors, Dr. Bergel gave me Norman Cousin's, "Albert Schweitzer in Lambarene," an inspirational tract and biography in one, with a lovely dedication. She could not know then, nor did I know, that one day I would teach Asian-American Studies and Japanese language courses, in her former classrooms. Before that, however, I transferred from

ELAC to California State University at Los Angeles, not more than half a mile away from ELAC. I arrived there as a Home Economics major. However, my days as the prospective good housewife forever in training were behind me. I started taking a variety of upper division courses. Every time I did well, the respective teacher recommended strongly that I stay with and major in the subject. Those included widely divergent ones like microbiology, psychology, sociology and art. Whatever the subject would be, the one constant in my mind remained that I must be able to teach it. Along with all the other subjects, I took education courses to prepare myself for teaching. I graduated again with honors in art and got a secondary teaching credential.

8

You Ain't Whitey, Are Ya'?

For my first full-time teaching assignment, the Los Angeles Unified School District elected to send me to Brett Harte Junior High School in Watts. I was to teach art to grades seven, eight and nine as a long-term substitute. By way of introduction and preparation, the principal interviewed me the day before I was to start teaching. She began by telling me that several teachers before me left after teaching only a few weeks and she hoped I would not do the same.

"Why?" I asked.

Her answers were vague. I asked what equipment and materials I would have to work with. Like scissors, paper, glue and such.

"Equipment? Materials? We have neither," she said. "The main thing," she continued, "is to keep them busy."

"To keep them busy doing what with what?" I asked.

"Tearing up magazines," she replied. "Now go see the vice-principal, who will tell you everything else you need to know."

In the vice-principal's office, I met another lady who welcomed me warmly. Her advice?

"When you have trouble in your class, send a student with a note to Mr. Johnson."

"Who is Mr. Johnson," I asked.

"He was a football player, but is now our trouble shooter."

"What kind of trouble are we talking about?"

"Oh, just the usual …" she replied.

I found out on my first day in my classroom what the usual would be like.

Now, after seeing the vice-principal I made the rounds of the other art teachers' classes. I noticed that they did have some equipment and materials.

"Where did you get those?" I asked them.

"You just have to get them wherever you can," was their answer

"I am new here," I said, "could you share some of your things with me?" I pleaded.

Some felt sorry for me and let me have some paper, a pair of scissors and a bottle of glue. Thus fortified I returned the next morning to face my students in Watts. Nothing had, and nothing could have, prepared me for what lay ahead.

Driving from Alhambra into South Central Los Angeles three years after the Watts riots was already intimidating. Much has been said about the shocking differences between the affluent

Los Angeles suburbs and the frightful conditions in the downtown Black ghetto. I did not then know the word ghetto, but I was clearly driving into another world. On my way, well-kept houses and manicured lawns gave way to rundown projects, littered streets and vacant lots. Everywhere groups of idle youths hung around checking out, I thought, who was coming into their turf.

It was the time of Black Power, Black Is Beautiful, Afro hairdos and racial consciousness. I had not paid much attention to this. I had no time to watch TV. My social life was limited and did not include Afro-American friends. I was not anti-Black. I just knew next to nothing about Blacks.

On my first day, I walk into my class and all students are Black, with the exception of one Mexican-American. I make my way to my desk walking as tall as I can manage. No one takes notice. Forty students mill around shouting obscenities, throwing things and sometimes each other through the air. Some girls in gym clothes are "visiting." I start calling the roll.

"Gloria Atkins!"

"Yeah!" comes the answer from one of the "visitors."

"Please be seated and listen!" I say calmly.

No one pays the slightest attention.

"Sit down and BE QUIET!" I shout.

"Did you say something?" one or two students volunteer.

"I am going to teach you something about art," I scream back.

I had come prepared with lesson plans and visual aids. This first day I was going to teach my class about colors. As a semblance of calm settled over the class, I brought out my chart with three interlocking circles of red, blue and yellow, the primary colors. I started to explain that the overlapping parts of the circle contained secondary colors.

"What's that got to do with us? What are we gonna DO?"

"What would YOU like to do?"

"Noth'n!"

"In that case," I said, let's draw a face. Your own face."

"How do we know what we look like?"

"Draw what you THINK you look like!"

I drew a picture of an egg on the blackboard and explained that they could use this as a basis.

"Most people have eyes and ears and mouths in certain places."

I filled in the egg on the blackboard accordingly. Some students started to rise to this challenge. Others followed. I asked them to sign their names on the back of their papers so that I would be able to return them the next day. At the end of the period, I collected their drawings. I had made it through the hour without serious incidents. I was not fully aware then, but suspected correctly that this would be an achievement in and of itself every day.

The next day I walk into the same melee. I make my way to my desk. A muscular boy is sitting on the desk with his back toward me.

He looks over his shoulder and says, "Hey babe! How 'bout a date?"

"Get off my desk! I'm a black belt in Karate. If you lay one finger on me, I'm gonna split you in half!" I hiss.

As the boy jumps off the desk, others take notice.

"Hey," I heard one of them say. "She all right!"

However, there were problems for which no teachers' training could have prepared me. Like illiteracy. When I tried to return their first assignments, I turned the papers to read off their names. All were marked with an X. Could it be that they cannot write their own names? Yes, it could. Their first assignment, the drawings of their faces, now became their logo. How could this be? How could my students, born and raised in America, have passed through elementary school and be enrolled in junior high school without learning how to write their names? I began to see their truculence and impossibly destructive behavior in a new light. But I had actually seen nothing yet.

One day the real Gloria Atkins for whom another girl had answered roll call the first day, came to me after class and asked if she could stay with me for the rest of the day in all my classes.

"Why?" I asked her. She did not answer.

"I'm sorry; I cannot keep you unless you tell me what's going on."

Without a word, she raised her skirt and showed me the inside of her thigh. There were two cigarette burns on both sides.

"How did this happen?"

"Two girls did it."

"Which two girls?"

I forgot the first-day "visitors" in gym clothes, whom I had reported to the vice-principal. Those girls got even.

"They lynched me," said Gloria.

When I tried to send her to the nurse's office, I learned that there were no nurses on duty at our school.

"Black Panthers!" A shout in the middle of a class.

Everyone ran outside to see what was going on. I stayed inside alone. The time to call Mr. Johnson had arrived. He came and rounded up my students and brought them back inside.

"Against the wall!"

Hands raised, rear ends turned towards Mr. Johnson, the boys obeyed as though waiting to be frisked. Suddenly I was in one of those American movies about juvenile delinquents.

Mr. Johnson walked along the line of boys briskly whacking each one on the behind with a wooden paddle. Like a drill sergeant, he reminded them that this was just a sample of what lay in store for them all, if they did not behave. For once there was an almost eerie silence. It did not last. No sooner had Mr. Johnson left the classroom than chaos returned. The boys who had been punished broke into a victory dance wearing their public reprimands like badges of honor.

Once, a former Japanese High School classmate came to visit my class. He was writing an article about Black heritage for a Japanese magazine. Halfway through the hour, two girls started a fight. Within seconds, they were on the ground pounding each other and pulling hair. Everyone rose to cheer them on.

There were the incidents with the BB guns. One of my girl students took to shooting at me every time my back was turned to the class. I confiscated the gun. She returned with a new one the next day. This continued for several days.

I turned in a report to the vice-principal and got a reply that said, "Three swats."

Was I to give her three swats? Had she gotten three swats? I never found out. However, I began to understand what my colleagues meant when they described teaching in inner city schools as combat duty, albeit without combat pay.

Brett Harte Junior High School did, in fact, often resemble a combat theater. On any normal day trashcans would explode. Rocks would crash through classroom windows. Parked cars would be stripped. Administrators routinely locked themselves into their offices. I taught in a bungalow separated from the main building. I locked myself in, also.

Fear became my constant companion, occasionally interrupted by emergency meetings. That meant something of special seriousness had happened or was going on. There was the meeting about the Mr. Johnson matter, the man we all relied upon to protect us from the worst. Five high school dropouts had attacked Mr. Johnson with knives. He was in the hospital in serious condition. Already, however, he was being sued by the parents of one of his attackers, whom he had hit with a baseball bat in self-defense.

The attack on Mr. Johnson was a turning point for me. I had now taught for three months. I had made some progress in teaching my students art and art appreciation. I had even developed some rapport with some of them. Our last project had been to make Christmas decorations and to prepare a tree for the holiday program in the assembly hall. As a present to my students, I had bought origami paper and glitters. Our tree turned out beautifully. My students had their logos on their creations. I was touched by the pride with which they showed their "art" to their parents. As I walked out of the building, I passed our Christmas tree. The tree was standing bare. All our decorations had been stripped off.

The last day before Christmas vacation I cleaned out my classroom cabinet. I returned all the material and grade books to the principal and said, "I am not coming back."

"It's going to inconvenience us," she said with a resigned shrug of her shoulders.

It may have been a matter of inconvenience for the school, but I knew it was a matter of survival for me. I had lived in a state of siege. I would get up and feel nauseated. I would drive onto the campus and walk like a warrior into enemy territory. All day I was in combat mode with my defenses up. I would arrive home shaking. Every day, I thanked my ancestors for having watched over me another day.

This was not what I had come to America for. This was not why I had become a teacher. Working in a ghetto school as an outsider in more ways than one, I was destined to fail. Failure and defeat were not in my plans. In retrospect, I can only marvel at the thoughtlessness of school administrators who would assign a Japanese girl, fresh out of college, not yet an American citizen, to an almost all-Black junior high school in an almost all-Black ghetto of inner city Los Angeles.

Later, in my Asian Studies courses, I would deal with the term "culture shock." Teaching in Watts had given me personal experience. I was as shocking to my students there as they were to me. I had never been in close contact with large numbers of Blacks. They had never been close up to a Japanese.

One of my Black students asked me, "You ain't whitey, are ya'?"

"No, I'm not."

"You pinky?"

"Pardon me? What's pinky?"

"Them part black part white."

"I see. I am Japanese."

"What's that?"

"It is one of the Asian people."

"Asian? Where you from?"

"Japan."

"Where's that?"

"It's an island nation. I'm going back there for Christmas vacation."

"On the bus?"

9

You Are Chinese, Aren't You?

My next call for long-term sub came at the beginning of the following spring semester. I was to report to Le Conte Junior High School in Hollywood. On my first day, I drove the Hollywood Freeway to Sunset Boulevard. The High School is located directly behind the KTLA Station building. My assignment was to teach design and crafts. From the parking lot on to the hallways, the atmosphere was one of casual opulence.

I found my large classroom with a spacious walk-in closet attached and stocked with all the materials I might want to use. At one end of the closet was a professional ceramist's kiln. Along the windows ran counters where students could work with small electric kilns and cutting boards. Large workbenches filled the rest of the room.

In Watts, I had just walked into my class every morning and started teaching. In Hollywood, I was assigned a homeroom in which I was to lead a group of students in reciting the pledge of allegiance every morning before classes started. These were not the students I was to teach. I would ask one of the students to lead the recital. Everybody put their right hand on their heart and spoke in unison, while I bowed my head in silence with my hands clasped in front of me. On my second day, I was called to the principal's office.

"Why don't you salute the flag of the United States?" he wanted to know.

"Because I am not a citizen of the United States. Would you salute the flag of a foreign country?"

"Of course not."

Then he explained. One of my homeroom student's father was a high ranking member of the John Birch Society. His daughter had reported to him that a "Communist Chinese" was teaching at her school. The John Birch Society had been founded to combat World Communism in general and Communist influence and infiltration in American schools in particular.

"I am furious that you would let a Chinese Communist teach my daughter!" the principal quoted the father.

"You are Chinese, aren't you?"

"No, I am not."

"What are you then?"

"Japanese."

"I see."

I asked the principal to explain to the enraged father that I had signed a statement of intention to become a US citizen as part of my requirements to teach in an American public school. I was in the clear and had no intentions to undermine the American government or subvert the minds of my students.

In Watts, I had gotten a brief introduction to a culture of poverty. In Hollywood, I was about to experience a world at the other end of the economic spectrum. Many of my students were chauffeured to school in expensive cars or limousines. They walked self-assuredly in their up-to-date fashions. They had the self-confidence that comes with privilege and exposure to travel and life in high society. They were namedroppers already. Two students stand out in my mind. There was Phillip the seventh grader who dressed like a prince in a Shakespearean play, ruffles, crotch pouch and all. I asked him to explain his "modern art" painting.

"This represents the liquidation of our society," he replied with the sophistication of a Louvre docent.

Taking my cue from my students, I said, "Far out!"

Later I learned that Phillip's mother was a famous modern artist. The other student was Veronica, a beautiful ninth grader, a 15-year-old passing for 28 or older. When she swept into the classroom, dressed in flowing theatrical garments, the boys were drawn to her like moths to the light. She was a star. I tried to ignore this sideshow, but art and I were the losers. There were many days Veronica did not appear. That's when I delivered her homework to one of the lesser Hollywood studios.

When I reported this to the girls' vice-principal, she said to me, "Oh yes, Veronica! Isn't she a bitch?" And we laughed.

If students had private matters to discuss, I would take them into the walk-in closet. No one could look in or out. No one could hear us.

Here a girl came to me one day and said, "I am not feeling well. Can I be excused?"

"What is wrong?" I asked.

"I guess I'm pregnant," she said matter-of-factly.

I had no experience with this sort of problem before. In my high school days in Japan, teen pregnancy was unheard of. I sent the girl to the campus nurse. Le Conte Junior High did, of course, have a fully equipped nursing staff.

Another girl came in very upset and said, "I was raped by my stepfather."

Another case for the nurse. In fact, coming from a culture in which interpersonal relationships in general are more restrained and restricted and the relationship between teacher and student is particularly prescribed and rigorously regulated, I found such encounters involving intensely private matters daunting.

In the middle of my semester in Hollywood, the Teachers' Union went on strike. I was a long-term sub and not a member of the union. I did not participate in the strike. This meant crossing the picket line as I arrived for work in the morning.

Already in the parking lot, the striking teachers waved their placards at me and shouted, "Don't cross the line! Go home!"

One teacher leaned in my car window, "Are you against us?"

I said, "No, but I need the money to survive. Your union doesn't support part-timers."

I crossed the line and went to my class. Very few students showed up. In some classes, no students had come in. There was little work to do and the teachers who had come to teach gathered to do some soul-searching. This was my introduction to union management politics as it is played in America. I understood that I was asked to make sacrifices in the long-term interest of union members. Today I know that this was actually an unfair demand to make. Part-time teachers and long-term subs were then, and are not now, union members and not covered by union contracts. They are the exploited multitude of teachers that the unions have, in fact, left out in the cold.

The strike ended in time for all to come together for graduation ceremonies. I was asked to give art awards to some of my outstanding students. My choice was a Chinese girl, whose overall performance, I believed, had been the best. She had a competitor, who did not take my selection well. This girl had been promised by the teacher I replaced that she would get the award if she completed a large papier-mâché horse. The horse did not impress me as much as it did her enraged parents, who came to me after the ceremony to tell me how unfair my choice had been.

"You are prejudiced. Just because YOU are Asian, you think you are better!"

10

Go Home And Have Children

Teaching in Watts and Hollywood in the turbulent late 1960's I consider one of the most valuable experiences in my Americanization. Moreover, it also made me realize that teaching at high schools was not for me. I wanted to teach students who wanted to learn rather than to face teenagers naturally bent on testing their teachers every day. I did not enjoy the disciplinary duties that come with public high school teaching. I also realized that I would never be able to adapt well or completely to the comparative permissiveness in American public schools. My own life passing through Japanese public schools had been one of extreme discipline. I could not help resenting the casual disrespect and mischievous treatment American secondary teachers are used to.

I had also discovered that I did not want to teach art. I enjoyed the creative part of it, but teaching it was another matter. Most students, and presumably their parents, thought of art as no more than having fun and horsing around. Evaluating and grading artwork of my students gave me endless headaches.

How do you teach to be innovative and artistic and then judge the results objectively? At that time the specialization in oriental art history, which I had wanted to pursue for a masters degree, did not exist. There were no faculty members trained and able to supervise a thesis in this field at California State University at Los Angeles (CSULA). A friend of mine, who had gotten her degree in art history from University of California at Los Angeles (UCLA) and then could not find a job, advised me strongly to look elsewhere.

I started my search during summer vacation. Looking for a second chance to transfer to UCLA I went there to explore their Oriental Languages Department. I loved the campus, but their requirements would have set me back two years. I tried my luck at USC (University of Southern California). Here I asked Dr. Thompson, the chairman of the Asian Studies Department, what USC might have to offer.

Reclining in his chair with his legs resting on his desk and smoking a pipe, Dr. Thompson said between puffs, "Well, if I were you, I would go home and have children."

This kind of rudeness and casual male chauvinist piggishness was already under siege, but this chairman had not received the word, as yet. I said nothing and left. This time I was not crying. I knew by now that such thoughtless stupidity would have to be and could be overcome. It was the mantra intoned all around me. As it turned out, Dr. Thompson was overcome sooner than

I could have hoped. Before the fall semester started, Dr. Mieko Han had replaced him as chairperson of the Asian Studies Department at USC. I had met Dr. Han when I was teaching at the local Japanese school in Monterey Park. We were using her textbooks.

Through the Japanese networking I mentioned earlier, I had gotten my first teaching job shortly after becoming a student at ELAC. It involved teaching Japanese to the third generation Japanese Americans, *Sansei,* once a week on Saturdays. These sessions were held at the Montebello Congregational Church, whose membership was mostly Japanese-American. Among other things, this supplemented my weekly stipend of five dollars at the Wilson household. I had also been asked by members of the Methodist Church in Monterey Park to establish a new Japanese school for children and adults who were interested in learning Japanese. I became the founder and first teacher. The school has lasted over three decades. My first students are now parents themselves, and some of their children are in attendance.

However, attitudes and demography change. There has always been a tendency among immigrant groups in America to want to lose their mother language, starting in the second generation and accelerating in the third. This is now also apparent at my school in Monterey Park as well as East Los Angeles College. There are more other Asian and non-Asian students studying Japanese than Japanese-Americans. The motivation for studying Japanese has shifted from learning and maintaining the language for cultural reasons to acquiring a basic knowledge of it for commercial purposes or personal interest.

Back to USC. In Dr. Han, I had met the one person in America who would have the deepest and most lasting influence in my professional career. She was a pioneer in Japanese language and the author of one of the first academically recognized Japanese language textbooks. She taught at UCLA before she was asked to come to USC as a full professor. She offered me a teaching assistantship. I met some of the other graduate students in the department at an orientation party.

"I hear you are the new protégé of Dr. Han," one of them said. "Prepare yourself, you'll soon find out what life is like in our ivory tower."

"What might I find out?" I asked.

"For example that you'll be working for a professor with a well deserved reputation as a slave driver. We call her the Black Widow. She is very hard to please. Don't ever cross her. You could not win. She always comes out smelling like a rose."

My relationship with Dr. Han became a symbiotic one. I received intellectual guidance, advice and unwavering support for my master's thesis. In return, I prepared and taught all of Dr. Han's undergraduate Japanese courses, did all the grading, wrote all letters of recommendation, drew pictures for the visual aids we used at that time, while also working towards and completing my own coursework. Dr. Han's trust and confidence in my performance as a student and teacher gave me the strength and self-confidence to get through my workdays at very low pay.

At USC, I was inside the ivory towers of academia. I had arrived at the advanced seminar level. As a teaching assistant, I sat in faculty meetings as a non-voting member of the USC Asian Studies Department. It was a small department, in which the "takeover" by Dr. Han had caused a stir. The defeated Dr. Thompson was plotting his comeback. One of the first lessons in intradepartmental politics I learned here was that there tends to be a division and ongoing struggle between those who are qualified to teach culture and language classes and teach them well, and those who are not and do not.

On both sides, alliances are formed to protect vested interests and one another. At the Asian Studies Department at USC those divisions existed at the time I was there. One day I witnessed one of its most shocking manifestations. We were all assembled for a regular department meeting. Dr. Han, the chair, was reading an announcement, when the other members began leaving the room one after the other. We could see them congregating in the hallway. Dr. Han stopped reading as a delegate passed a note to her from the members outside the room.

Trembling she announced, "I have just been given notice that the members voted to replace me as the chair."

As the teaching assistants sat in stunned silence, Dr. Han gathered her papers and left. We followed her, avoiding eye contact with the conspirators in the hallway. No one spoke a word. It would be two years, before Dr. Han would win her lawsuit against the university. For Dr. Han it had been a valiant struggle. For me, it was an eye opener. Behind an intellectual façade bickering, politicking, kowtowing, badmouthing, back-stabbing and petty jealousies are alive and well. It did not, however, quite prepare me for the time I became a "victim" myself.

In 1972 after graduating from USC I began teaching at the University of California at Irvine, (UC Irvine) the newest of the ten University of California campuses. The teaching load was light, but we were expected to do research, publish and be active in community affairs. When I arrived there, it had a ranch feeling to it, because it was built on one. The Irvine Company had donated the land and there was lots of it. Buildings were arranged in a circle like the covered wagons of the pioneers with a large park in the middle. Distances between classrooms were long. Rabbits and squirrels greeted you on your way. Students in the buff, "streakers" as they came to be known, might play a game of Frisbee. Others napped on the grass in the shade of the 200 ornamental cherry trees donated by sister city Matsue in Japan.

I was shown into my office with a picture window giving a view over cows grazing and vast open space. I had a nicely furnished office all to myself. All classrooms were new and air-conditioned. Meeting rooms were more like elegant executive lounges with never a coffee maker missing or out of working order.

If my schoolmates in Japan could see me now! As a matter of fact, when I showed pictures of UC Irvine, to family and friends in Japan, they thought I must have my office and be teaching on a golf course.

11

Where Are The Wives?

Almost as soon as I arrived in UC Irvine, I was approached by the Irvine Company to assist them in their drive to attract Japanese companies to Orange County. What would attract Japanese executives to make such a decision? The Irvine Company was prepared to offer a completely planned community. But what needed to be planned? What would the Japanese like, need, or insist on? How could a Japanese family be made comfortable in the vastness of Orange County? How could they be helped to adjust to American culture?

I began my consulting work with a translation into Japanese of the most important telephone numbers and services that the Japanese arriving in Irvine might need. Such instructions printed in several languages were then a rarity. I designed an English language course for Japanese taught by native English speakers. This course was to be taught along with my culture courses, to introduce the Japanese to the American way of life. I suggested to the Irvine Company that in their designs for housing the Japanese, rather than one big all-purpose recreation hall, an *idobata kaigi*, an around-the-well meeting area be included. This is where Japanese housewives gossip, network, and discuss problems among themselves. Of course, there would be no well like in old Japan. However, the custom of getting together in a village center is still strong in Japan, even in many small neighborhoods in large cities such as Tokyo. In a large hall, Japanese do not feel comfortable. We say, "The step is too high" to get in. Some of those problems could be strange from a Western perspective, but very serious for the Japanese.

One such situation arose when I was asked by a local Orange County magazine to recommend one of the new Japanese families for a cover story to acquaint the American readers with their new neighbors, their customs, culture and way of life. I picked the family of a woman who had volunteered to be a tutor in my Japanese classes in return for a chance for her to be among English speaking people and experience American college life. The story in the local magazine was a great success with American readers but a disaster with the Japanese, in particular with the family I had chosen to be spotlighted. Gossip at the *idobata* went into high gear. "Why them?" was the big question to which no Japanese could find an answer. "Her husband is only a manager, not the president of the company!" In terms of hierarchy, a major *faux pas* had been committed. I took care not to advertise too broadly that I had been the cause of it. However, I spent quality time with my tutor, who was near a nervous breakdown after the article appeared and her neighbors descended upon her mercilessly.

In my evening courses for the Japanese executives, my most enthusiastic students were the vice-president of the company and his wife. After a few weeks they stopped attending class. I tried to find out what had happened. At first I got only vague answers, but then someone told me directly, "The president of the company is not attending your class, is he?"

There are the subtle cultural misunderstandings that no amount of planning and goodwill can predict or prevent. The Irvine Company experiment was generally well planned and approached with generosity and genuine good will by all involved on both sides. Yet, every so often Irvine executives would come to me, throw up their hands and say: "Kay, what is going on? What do these Japanese want? Haven't we done enough? Why are they still complaining?"

By all business and social standards, the Irvine Company had done well. They had provided more than decent housing in a convenient and beautiful location. In addition, it made available an exceptionally wide range of services for free, that many Americans would envy. What did the Japanese complain about? What were the things they had come to demand? The Japanese looked at the offer of free English and culture courses and said, "If they are free, they are probably not so good." If they were asked to pay, they hesitated, because they felt they should be provided for them without charge. The logic in this circular argument was lost on their American hosts.

Social gatherings were another area of contention. If there was a party, all the Japanese men would come without their wives as they are used to do in Japan.

The American executives asked me, "Kay, where are their wives? The invitation clearly said 'you and your wife,' for Christ's sake!"

"Japanese men do not want their wives there, and the wives don't want to be there."

"You're kidding! Whoever heard of such a thing? If I asked my wife to stay home, she'd have a fit and I'd be hearing from her lawyer!"

"Not in Japan."

Again, I explained the crucial importance of hierarchy. What if the Japanese executives brought their wives and one of the lower ranking ones was better looking, better dressed, wore more jewelry than the higher ranking ones? That could not only ruin their evening but the husband's career as well. Why take the risk? Better stay with the children secure in one's role as the good and dutiful mother.

The Americans did not give up easily. An offer was made to have a babysitter take care of all the children, so that the Japanese could socialize as couples. That offer was accepted under certain conditions that brought the Americans running to my office for more advice and consolation.

"Kay, you won't believe this. They'll accept the babysitter, if we provide taxis to pick them up. And that's not all. They don't want to do it in the evening. Any explanation?"

"Ok, on the taxi. Most of the Japanese women don't drive. They are used to take public transportation. The idea of ordering a taxi themselves is seen as unnecessarily wasteful especially for housewives, who have only their husband's money to spend."

"Ok, what about meeting during the day then?"

"This is more difficult. You must try to understand that in Japan husbands and wives rarely go out in public together to have a good time. Partly, this is because Japanese men and women do different things when they want to have fun or relax. Partly, both men and women feel more relaxed among their peers. Partly, this also has to do with men working all day and expecting to be served by their wives when they come home."

"So, Kay, are you telling us that there is no way to have a party where the Japanese will attend in couples?"

"Well ..."

It was difficult to explain why these *shoosha,* Japanese sent for limited assignments to foreign countries, cannot step out of their own cultural boundaries and limitations and liberate themselves when they work in more open societies. They know they will return to Japan and they and their whole family must be able to fit in again as though they had never been away. If this was crucial and a challenge for the Japanese parents we dealt with in Irvine, it was equally imperative for their children not to become too Americanized, lest they be ostracized upon their return to their home country.

The situation was equally strained but much more hilarious when the Japanese tried to do the social thing for their American counterparts. Towards the end of the semester of free courses, I proposed to my Japanese executives and their wives that it might be well to show their appreciation to their hosts by inviting them to a Japanese potluck dinner, a new concept for the Japanese. Usually, in Japan guests are invited out to fancy restaurants.

Invitations went out. Counting all the American couples we had sent them to, we expected about 50 people to come. The Japanese prepared small portions of delicate food for 50. They wrapped everything exquisitely and served it in beautiful containers. As the Americans arrived and introduced the often many members of their family, it became clear that there would not be enough food. Hoping against hope, I welcomed them and asked them to help themselves.

The Americans rushed forward like an invading army and cleared the plates in record time. All the Japanese had hung back in polite hesitation, *enryo*, realizing too late that there would be no dinner for them that night, while the Americans loaded their plates, albeit with a touch of suspicion, with food they had not tasted before. While they gingerly picked through the Sushi and Oden, the Tempura and Teriyaki, I was getting hungrier and angrier. In a panic, I ordered in an emergency supply of pizzas and spaghetti with salad. All that disappeared, too, as soon as it was delivered.

Food, as it turned out, was not the only thing that disappeared that evening. All the organizers' purses left in the kitchen, mine included, were gone when the party was over. For the Japanese, this was a cultural lesson of a different kind. Japan is known around the world for its low crime rate. Stories of articles left behind but returned to their owner, often after considerable efforts irrespective of the value of the lost items, abound.

Our purses were never to be seen again.

12

The Year Of Calamity

✦

Yakudoshi

Every culture has its superstitions that enlightenment, modern science and high-tech have not been able to subdue, let alone erase. In Japan, one strongly held superstition is that for women age 33 and for men age 42 will be their years of calamity and misfortune. When my brother turned 42, he visited his local Shinto shrine to pray and throw coins at the four corners of the interior court. This might ward off the wrath of the evil spirits and alert our ancestors and gods to watch out for him.

For me, my 33rd year began with me cutting my finger on New Year's Day. That meant the upcoming year would be a very bad one. I also called on my dead ancestors, but they were not listening or were busy protecting my brother. I bandaged my finger and tried to forget about it.

A committee of community activists, who felt that Asian languages and culture should be included in the university's Comparative Culture Department, had requested my position as a lecturer at UC Irvine. I was hired to teach Japanese language and Asian cultures. Those were popular courses with high enrollment for the entire time I taught them. My students' evaluations were the highest in the department. I enjoyed what I was doing. I had a wonderful rapport with my students and colleagues. I was on top of the world.

One day in my third year of teaching, just before Thanksgiving holiday, a department meeting was called. Budget cuts had been announced, and rumors were circulating that layoffs were imminent. As we took our comfortable chairs in the comfortable department lounge, the atmosphere was one of unease.

Our chairman, Dr. Jorgensen, in an attempt to break the ice, opened the meeting by saying, "All of you are invited to a Thanksgiving dinner! The question is which one of you turkeys will be cooked."

No one laughed.

"Some of you will receive March 15th letters."

"Can you be more specific?"

"Not at this time."

No one spoke as we made our way to our offices and closed the door behind us, something we had never done before. A group of congenial colleagues were now competitors—suspicious of each other. No group spirit developed to face the impending disaster together. The Comparative Culture Department was multiethnic in course offerings and in its teaching staff. A superficial mutual tolerance had developed among us. This changed when the actual layoffs were announced. A division opened up between the ones who had received their March 15 letters and those who had not. I was one of the former. I was also the only one who decided not to take this lying down.

I began by telling my students that the courses they were taking would be cut from the course schedule and that I was being terminated as of the end of the quarter. My students rallied around me. They collected 2000 signatures on a petition. They composed a written rational for why the courses in Japanese language and culture courses should be continued. They held meetings and public rallies on campus. They explained their views in the campus newspaper. They canvassed community organizations for their support. They formed a committee and met with UC Irvine administrators. I met with the Vice Chancellor of Academic Affairs and the Chancellor as well as the director of the Affirmative Action program.

"I have a long shopping list," said the white Vice Chancellor of academic affairs, "but Japanese is not on that list."

"Why is it not on the list," I asked, "when enrollment is high and increasing from quarter to quarter?"

"If we have four students in Greek and Latin," the Vice Chancellor explained, "we'll keep those courses, because they are important academic courses."

"And Japanese and Asian Culture courses are not that important?" I asked.

"Yes, that's what I am saying."

The white Chancellor echoed the Vice Chancellor's views but added this insight, "The only reason students are taking Japanese courses is that they want to get a job with Mazda or Toyota. Let those companies pick up the tab!"

The Latino gentleman in charge of Affirmative Action said to me, "Our hands are tied."

"Does that mean you will not do anything about this?"

"Essentially, yes."

He was himself a token minority employee with no power but an understandable healthy interest in keeping his own job. The same was true for the black Chancellor for student affairs who told me with an air of confidentiality, "If I were you, I'd just lay low and go and stay home."

"Lay low while I'm laid off?"

What hurt, but should not have surprised me, came from other senior Japanese faculty members whom I approached for support.

"Don't make the water muddy, while you are flying away!" was their proverbial advice.

Meaning well, but also in self-interest no doubt, they cautioned, "When you go for your next job, you want to have good recommendations. Don't spoil your chances!"

What they all had in the back of their minds was the Japanese concept of *haji,* which simply means putting shame and blame on the victim for making trouble.

A friend suggested that I come with her to a meeting of other women who had formed one of the Women's Liberation Movement groups that had then sprung up all over the country. I was skeptic. I had not followed the movement very closely, but knew that one of the main goals of the members was burning their bras and to get the men in their lives and men in general to do housework and diaper the babies. Other headlines that attracted my cursory attention had dealt with women fighting to work in coalmines. I could not identify with any of this, but what could I lose by attending one of their meetings?

As I walked into the meeting room, I was engulfed in a sea of T-shirts, many of them screaming aggressive messages across front and back and covering bra-liberated breasts. Worn jeans and unkempt hair rounded out the picture of the women who seemed to go out of their way to demonstrate how relaxed and definitely not other, that is male, directed they were.

To say that I was overdressed would be an understatement—high heels, hose, professional suit, makeup and every hair in place, neat purse by my side, good posture. To this challenge, the women rose with alacrity. Where was I from, they wanted to know. In other words, where was that place where women like me still existed? Who told me how to dress? What was all that makeup for? Whom was I trying to impress? And the *coup de grâce*—that PURSE! When was the last time they had traipsed around dangling purses? Not one of them could remember. I felt uncomfortable. I could not see what, other than gender, I could have in common with these women. The idea that they would take up my "cause" against the male dominated university was ludicrous. Another dead end. By the end of the spring quarter I was unemployed.

The shock of being out of work was deep and complete. Suddenly, there was no reason for me to get out of bed in the morning. The rigorous but pleasant structure in my life had collapsed as though washed away by a tsunami. Lying on my couch reading willy-nilly to occupy myself, I had a feeling as though I was rotting from within. Against better judgment, I felt ashamed. I stayed by myself to avoid having to explain my situation and the pity that might be coming my way. I had to force myself to apply for unemployment compensation. The Asian work ethic does not provide much room for government handouts. It is like begging. It is demeaning. It is admitting failure. My American colleagues, I found, had less problem presenting their pink slips and collecting what they "had coming to them."

One day in line at the unemployment office in Santa Ana, in a working class neighborhood, the man in front of me in blue jeans and T-shirt with a pack of cigarettes rolled into one short sleeve, tattoos running up and down his arms, turned and said, "Time to get some cash, ain't it?"

"Yes."

"This your first time?"

"First time."

"What you been doing?"

"Teaching at UC Irvine."

"I thought you looked different."

"Yes? How so?"

"No one here with a suit like yours except the ones behind the counter."

"Old habit. What did you do?"

"This and that, whatever."

When it was my turn, a man in a brown suit began the interview. "Have you applied for any jobs already?"

"Yes I have."

"What happened?"

"Overqualified."

"I see. What are you qualified for?"

"Teaching."

"Teaching what?"

"Japanese language and Asian Studies."

"That'll be a tough one. Anything else you could do?"

"Consulting. Translating. Interpreting. Tour guide. That sort of thing."

"Well, keep looking. Nothing here today."

I got off my couch and began making the rounds. Within a week or two I had found a part-time teaching job at California State University Long Beach. I got a business license and formed my own consulting firm. Friends from the Irvine Company offered a free office. I moved in, designed and handwrote a pretty brochure, sent it to Japanese companies and distributed it to stores in the Japanese neighborhoods. The range of services I offered was exceptionally broad. It included all personal and family problems known to man, as well as business negotiations and immigration matters. Business was not brisk, to put it elegantly. Consulting, I learned to my chagrin, to most of my clients meant using me as a wailing wall, a place and person to unload and just talk to as they could not talk to anybody else. I listened, made phone calls, gave advice, made connections to social service agencies that might be of help. But whether I succeeded or not, the general attitude was that we had only talked, and why should they pay for it? Still, I had a reason to get out of bed in the morning. I had a business. I was busy. I felt good about helping people. They felt good about me.

There was, for example, the Japanese-speaking Korean woman whose husband abused her. I had to meet her in a secret location so the husband would not find out.

"How can I help you?" I asked looking at her battered face.

"My husband goes to the horse races with all the money from our gas station cash register. He loses all the money and then kicks and beats me up. The children try to stop him, but he is a Tae Kwon Do black belt."

"Do you want to divorce him? Do you want me to find a lawyer for you? It would cost you $300 in advance for his fee."

At our next meeting, she told me that her three children had each given her $100. We filed for divorce. I went as far as taking her $300 to the lawyer and gave the woman my apartment keys in case she needed a place to hide. On the date set for her court appearance, she did not show up. I never saw or heard from her again, nor did she pay me anything, of course.

I listed my name as an interpreter and translator with the Orange County courts. In that capacity, I translated and explained back and forth at depositions, ongoing court cases and accompanied public defenders to jail. There were virtually no Japanese speaking lawyers at that time. The pay was low. Translators, I found, do not have the financial clout of lawyers, although they are as crucial for orderly legal proceedings.

I signed up for a preparation course to pass the qualifying exam to law school. There should be a niche, I reasoned, for lawyers fluent in Japanese and English.

On the day I went to take the test, I had a high fever and the examiner said, "You better go home. You are in no condition to take this test." It turned out to be strep throat.

Today, every time I pass by the UC Irvine campus, I have strong but mixed feelings. Some of my best memories are here, but they are overshadowed by the catastrophe of being fired. For ten years after my departure, no Asian language or culture courses were offered at UC Irvine although Asian enrollment kept increasing.

Now, with more than half its student body of Asian extraction, a full program of Asian language and culture courses is offered. I nurse a degree of satisfaction for having been one of the program's pioneers. One of my former serious students, Judy Glickman Kimura, for whom I had arranged an extended scholarship to study in Japan, is now teaching Japanese at UC Irvine.

For me, the superstition of the year of calamity was fulfilled with a vengeance. However, it was to be followed by better years.

13

Coming Home To My Alma Mater

I have mentioned before the informal networking in the Japanese community in California. I had let the word go out that I was looking for a full-time job. Shortly, I heard from Dr. Yuri Han, husband of my mentor, Mieko Han, who taught at East Los Angeles College. There was an opening for an Asian specialist in their Title VII Program, one of the federally funded programs designed to develop bilingual teaching, an idea then in its infancy. It was a full-time position, though not in teaching, but a foot in the door at an institution that I loved. It was like a homecoming.

I moved into a bungalow that housed, behind open partitions, other programs that had one thing in common—their dependency on grant moneys from either local, state or federal agencies. Beyond that, we were motivated by the general goal of improving students' lives and academic performance. So was the California legislature, which had mandated that in classes with a minimum of 10 students who spoke the same language other than English, bilingual teachers should teach regular subjects other than languages. Such teachers would get extra pay for their efforts. Only rudimentary or no guidelines on how to teach such classes existed. This brought on a rash of workshops, often held in pleasant locations in or outside the state. One such affair I attended in New Orleans. An impressive offering of break out sessions was available, but attendance was usually low. Many of the government paid administrators and prospective bilingual teachers found time to explore the city and surroundings and to have a really good time.

The field of qualified applicants was narrow. I interviewed one applicant, who admitted that his Ph.D. was of the mail order kind. He spoke fluent Korean, but had no idea of how to teach it or any other subject in that language. This held true for other languages, also. An on-campus committee and a federal official investigated charges of misuse of funds. This led to the involuntary departure of some of the program directors, including my supervisor, and my elevation by default to take his place.

At East Los Angeles College, the head of the federally funded programs was a nephew of our college president. His girlfriend, Angela, became my secretary. She could not type and was prone to take two-week leaves without giving notice. This was not helpful at a time we were under deadline to write project proposals to secure continued funding. Though Angela was always welcomed back with roses from her protector, I fired her. I finished my proposals with outside help, and we got the money for which we applied. To this day, I have mixed feelings about my tenure as program director. As with so many government-funded initiatives, the underlying ideas and the goal to help disadvantaged students were good in a general way. What I found disappointing and, eventually, maddening, was the amount of effort that went into "administration" by everyone involved.

There was, for example, the cumbersome though largely ineffective hiring process that led to the employment of mostly people who had little or no knowledge or experience in the nascent fields of bilingual education and ethnic studies. Both were a response to demands made by student representatives in the late 60's, backed up by sit-ins and more violent demonstrations at universities across the country. Even East Los Angeles had had its "rumbles" in 1968 that ended with an occupation of the Ingalls Auditorium and the presentation of a list of demands to the president of the college. It was, therefore, largely to placate students' outrage, that colleges and universities rushed ethnic studies programs into operation. East Los Angeles College was not to be left behind. Interviews for a part-time position in Asian American studies were announced. I applied immediately. When the results were announced, I had been chosen over a part-time teacher who had already been teaching courses in this field at ELAC. He did not take it kindly. When the semester opened, he refused to vacate his desk. For weeks, I walked from class to class carrying all my course materials and rosters with me in a carton, while he used our office and typewriter to write poison letters about me to the Japanese newspaper *Rafu Shimpo* and others.

There were no standard course outlines or syllabi on Asian Studies' courses. I went to the Amerasia Bookstore in Little Tokyo and bought all their books dealing with Asian Americans and many more on Asian cultures, art and religions. Each new semester I introduced a new course until my program had expanded to seven courses, of which I taught five different ones at a time. The amount of preparation was enormous, and we had no teaching assistants.

All my classes came up to the minimum number of students, though some creative recruiting was necessary from time to time. This is where the networking helped greatly. By that time, I knew most instructors in the Los Angeles area, who had taught or were teaching similar courses, and they knew me. We had fought many battles together at UCLA, UC Irvine and USC. We had lost some and won some. We were not necessarily all close friends, but we had done favors for each other. That became the basis for an enduring system of mutual reliance and support and, this being a Japanese networking system, *giri*, that web of obligations, in times of need.

In due time, I received tenure as a full-time instructor at East Los Angeles College. That, according to common belief, should have taken the pressure and insecurity out of my professional life, as in most cases it does. I scraped together all my financial resources and bought a townhouse at high interest rates five minutes from ELAC campus. Then I learned that tenure can also be less than it is cracked up to be.

From the inception of the ethnic programs for Black, Latino and Asian students, these programs had been in competition with long established courses offered in the fields of history, sociology, political science, psychology, philosophy and others. Those disciplines argued that ethnic studies could and should be integrated into the accepted body of general knowledge that had made up the learning program of American schools and universities for so long.

Advocates and supporters of ethnic and women's studies, myself included, held that America had for too long taught all social science subjects from a deliberately and decidedly biased, narrow Anglo Western perspective. For most of America's history, this was comfortable for the Anglo White majority. It was thought to enhance and speed the Americanization of new arrivals. The educational establishment had accepted and internalized this view as the only way to achieve those two goals. US immigration laws, deliberately restrictive and discriminatory against Asians, and oriented towards admitting mostly people from Western Europe, had been the underpinning of this system.

In 1965, the United States Congress revised the country's immigration laws. That opened US borders to people from most countries in the world on a categories basis, in place of the quota system strongly slanted towards Western Europe. While immigration from Western Europe leveled off and began to decline, arrivals from Asian and Latin American countries began to soar.

For most Western Europeans, the switch from their mother tongues to English and from their European backgrounds to the "American Way of Life" did not involve deep culture shock. For Asians, it often does. European immigrants, therefore, generally found it easier to blend into the American population. The second generation usually felt, spoke, and looked like Americans. There were exceptions, of course, like New York City where German and Italian neighborhoods retained some of the old language and life styles.

By contrast and definition, it is vastly more difficult for Asian immigrants to blend in. However, most significant for schools and universities, many Asian families and their children born here now do not have a survival need to blend in. They have established their own large communities, where all services may be provided using their written and spoken mother languages. Monterey Park and others are thriving, commercially successful, examples. In Monterey Park, the city government passed an ordinance mandating English subheadings under Chinese, Vietnamese or Japanese store and market signs along the streets and shopping malls.

This development of sizable communities, functioning well using languages other than English, is also apparent among our college students. Here we have, in fact, gone from one extreme to another. In the past, it was common practice to punish children caught speaking a language other than English in school. Today at East Los Angeles College, more than forty foreign languages are spoken.

In many Asian cultures, the emphasis on education is strong with a bias towards skills that lead to making money. Yet, there is also a strong desire to pass on to the next generation the cultural and philosophical traditions of the former home countries. This is where Asian American Studies programs have their justification. In addition to imparting knowledge and history of Asian cultures and countries to Asian and non-Asian students, such programs and the teachers who teach them can help Asian students in particular with finding an identity in a competitive, Western-oriented society.

My hope for all students, Western and non-Western, is that the study of cultures other than their own can lead toward the deeper insight that there is no fundamental difference between "we" and "they." The study of cultures is the study of the ways in which all people are different and alike. At a time when *homo sapiens* has created weapons to destroy the species, this might yet become the most important reason to teach such courses. That realization does not, however, seem just around the corner. It speaks of the difficulty to bring about changes or introduce new ways of doing or teaching things in an entrenched educational system that the courses others and I had developed remain electives, which students can, but need not, take towards a well-rounded education.

My own struggle, as I already described, began in the early 1970's at UC Irvine. A second round of battles to save the Asian-American program at East Los Angeles College came at a time of general community college district reorganization in the early 1980's. At that time, I was teaching four courses of Asian American Studies and one class of Japanese Language. This was the time when enrollment of Asian students began to climb. The Asian economies were booming and supporting ever increasing numbers of foreign students on our campus. Many non-Asian students took my courses to improve their skills and chances to get jobs in Asian companies.

One day in 1986, out of the blue California sky, I received notice of termination for March 15, warning me that my employment at ELAC might end. The notice contained a list of courses that were to be reduced in number or eliminated altogether. The reorganization was to bring about a better balance of teaching talent among the nine campuses of the district. Where there were too many teachers in one subject, for example, some would have to be transferred to other campuses that were understaffed in that field. A number of volunteer and forced transfers were already taking place.

My case was different and, I imagine, somewhat troubling for the reorganizers. I was the only full-time instructor in the whole nine-campus district teaching Asian American Studies courses and Japanese language. Transferring me would hardly bring about a better balance. Once again, I was not prepared to take this lying down. I immediately contacted key community leaders, of whom I knew they shared my concerns. An informal committee of ten was formed that came to be known as "Committee to Save Asian-American Studies." Our first meeting took place in my house. Several community activists such as Alan Nishio, Glen Omatsu, Aki Maehara and others mapped out a strategy: inform the media; ask colleagues in the field to write letters of protest and support; contact Warren Furutani, who was running for the LAUSD Board of Trustees; collect donations to cover some of the costs.

I talked to Tricia Toyota, the anchorperson on a local network evening newscast. She was sympathetic, but did not feel our problems warranted a spot on her airtime. Articles about us appeared in local papers. ELAC students of Asian Studies were ready to rally. Support also came from students at UCLA, who collected small amounts of money for the cause. A number of concerned faculty members at ELAC individually talked to our Dean of Instructions, Mr. Robles. He, in turn, presented our protests to the Community College Board Members. The Board gave in. Our Asian American Studies program was to continue.

Shortly after we had won our fight at ELAC, news came down the networking pipeline from Glen Omatsu at UCLA that the efforts by the Asian American Studies Department to have Dr. Dan Nakanishi from the Education Department become its director, were being frustrated by Chancellor Robert Young, who was not willing to grant tenure to Dr. Nakanishi. On a minor note, moves were underway to relocate UCLA's Asian-American Studies Program to an unattractive basement.

Our time to repay our UCLA compatriots had arrived. About one hundred students, faculty and community supporters rallied for a candle light march to Chancellor Young's residence on campus. When I looked at the program, I noticed my name in print as one of the speakers. My topic was "East L.A. College—Victory." With emotion, I led my listeners through our defeat ten years before at UC Irvine to our victory at ELAC, "United we Win!" Everybody shouted when I had finished.

More speeches were made. Our feeling of empowerment grew by the minute, until we began to realize that Chancellor Young was not at home. In fact, no one was home. We left all our candles in front of the Chancellor's residence and went home with a feeling of accomplishment nevertheless. We did feel united and uplifted. We had made our point and the *Daily Bruin,* to its credit, wrote a report in its next morning's edition. Chancellor Young subsequently changed his mind. Dr. Nakanishi got tenure and became head of the Asian American Studies Department. Today, UCLA has one of the largest offerings in Asian American Studies leading to advanced degrees in this field.

It is very difficult to measure increases or decreases of tolerance of individuals or groups towards each other. I have no scientific data to prove possible trends in this area. Based on my own observations and intuition, however, I'm inclined to believe that among my students a modest broadening of intellectual horizons is taking place. When I first came to teach at ELAC, the general situation among Asian students was one of cliquishness. For example, there were Hong Kong Chinese, Mainland Chinese, Singaporean Chinese, Taiwanese Chinese and ABC's (American Born Chinese). There was little communication between them, let alone social intercourse. I founded the A.S.I.A. Club (Asian Students Intercultural Association). Here Asian students could meet and develop friendships with other students Asian and non-Asian alike. The Club has been thriving for many years. Formerly improbable close friendships have, indeed, been formed. The Club roster records several marriages that had their beginning here.

In my culture courses, I set out to explain and clarify the difference between stereotypes and common traits. For instance, the term "yellow skin" is the stereotype to describe the Asian "race" in general, while "black hair" is a common trait derived from a common Mongolian gene. One of the most difficult things I have found is to correct or erase stereotypes. Most people cannot explain where or from whom they got them, though none of us grows up without them. They are part and parcel of all cultures and as such are perpetuated and nurtured by society in general and the media and school systems in particular. In my classes, I confront students with their own, dearly held stereotypes and prejudices. It is likely that this is the first and last time they will be asked to make such an effort.

The aforementioned pro-Western bias in the social sciences in America began to change with Civil Rights and ethnic awareness movements in the 1960's. However, I found and still find that my students, both Western and Asian, come with little or no background in the history of Asians in America. For example, a matter as significant as the internment of all Japanese-

Americans on the U.S. West Coast in concentration camps for the duration of World War II, is generally either completely unknown or not understood from an Asian perspective. American textbooks treat this occurrence only as a necessity of national security.

Every semester I find that many of my students who take my Asian-American Studies classes have little or no knowledge of the "special treatment" Asian immigrants experienced in their daily lives in early America. Reactions among my non-Asian students vary. White students, a minority in those classes, feel uncomfortable when the topics come around to the deliberate and blatant discrimination Asian immigrants and American-born Asians have suffered in the United States in the past. At least one of my students wanted to drop the class, because he felt his Asian classmates appeared to hold him personally responsible. This reminded me of the time when I was taking an American History class and the Japanese attack on Pearl Harbor came up.

One of my classmates looked at me and yelled, "Remember Pearl Harbor!"

For some of my Asian students learning the history of Asians in America can be like self-analysis. They begin to realize intellectually and emotionally that they and their families are, indeed, part of this great American experiment to which their ancestors have already made significant contributions and sacrifices. Some of these students know more about their own countries and cultures than American-born students both Asian and non-Asian. They become my resource persons and we share their knowledge with the other students.

A good many students enroll in my Asian Studies classes for practical reasons. They have problems of all kinds and are looking for help or counseling. There are students with drug problems that have a cultural basis or explanation. While making their way through the American school system, their being Asian has alienated them from other students. This is compounded by their parents' attempts to turn them into good Asian kids in manners, dress and all the way to homemade Asian box lunches.

Other problems involve the generation gap and the rejection of traditional Asian culture by Americanized Asian kids. This is a problem that is not limited to Asian American students. I cannot, of course, play parent to all of my students, but I listen and share relevant experiences in my life with them. When the enrollment in my Asian American Studies classes was smaller than it has now become, I used to invite the whole class to my house for a potluck party once during each semester. One semester, I had a few members of the *Wah Ching* gang in my class. Fear spread through the house as they walked in. The other students huddled together in one small room, while the gang took over the rest of the house.

"Please take off your shoes!" I ordered.

"Oh, no Ma'am. Those are expensive shoes. We feel naked without them."

"In a Japanese home, you take off your shoes! Over there in the corner please!"

Reluctantly all gang members pulled off their boots—their symbols of power, as I well knew.

I pinned the leader, a man roughly twice my size to the wall and said, "I hold you fully responsible if anything is broken or stolen. And one more thing. Don't touch my liquor cabinet!"

"Yes Ma'am."

Gang members and the other students did not mix. At the end, the gang leader reported to me, "Ma'am, nothing broken, nothing stolen," as he and the others put on their shoes and left as a group.

There was a sigh of relief from the students who stayed to help me clean up. Two weeks later, my house was broken into and all my valuables were stolen. The police thought the place had been cased earlier.

When I mentioned the party with gang members present, the officer said, "No more parties!"

My colleagues echoed this order. "You give parties to students in your home?" they asked. "Do you trust them?"

I did and I still do.

14

The Eyes Can Be Fixed

When I was growing up in Japan, the sexual revolution had not occurred. Sex was not a topic in my family. It was not a topic in school. Revelatory talk shows had not arrived. How-to sexual manuals were not available. Openly pornographic, but also instructional, comic books were yet unknown. How was I to learn about sex?

There was *kimi no na wa?* Loosely translated this title of a radio soap opera means, "what's your name?" This show ran daily, and a large part of the Japanese population arranged its life around it. The show involved Machiko, the heroine, who is sought after by an improbably handsome suitor Haruki. An endless string of circumstances and fateful happenings combine to keep the lovers separated. Later, the soapsuds were whipped into a movie. In one particular scene that stuck in my mind, the couple passes each other in two trains going in opposite directions. They exchange soulful glances across the tracks. My heart ached as those trains moved past each other. Machiko also started a fashion trend of wearing shawls slung around her head and shoulders like Audrey Hepburn in "Sabrina."

Love and sex, in other words, were something completely abstract, something for movie stars. It had no meaning for us in real life. There was no one we could talk to, nor anything practical we could read. But we were, of course, curious teenagers, going through puberty. We devised clever, inconspicuous ways to make "contact" with the opposite sex. There were, for example, our "footnotes." Each one of the students, male and female, had assigned shoeboxes at the entrance to the school hallway. That's where we changed from outside shoes to inside slippers. That is where we girls slipped little notes to the boys and they to us. It was a thrill to guess who the sender of the notes might be. Often the notes bore false or no names. To find out, we used a small mirror in class to detect who among the boys might be looking at us.

It is an understatement to say that I was unprepared for American dating games and customs. Concepts such as going steady, and starting to do so in junior high school at the latest, were foreign to me. Spending time in lovers' lanes necking and petting and being generally bodily "close," I could not identify with. I had been cautioned to keep my distance, and that was meant literally. When I happened to be in a car with a boy, I would sit as close to the door as was humanly possible without becoming part of the door, my hand on the door handle ready to get out at a moment's notice. In my mind, I had my samurai sword ready to cut off heads. Trying to be helpful, my sponsors arranged a few blind dates for me. I wasn't entirely sure what blind meant, but it sounded vaguely reassuring.

My first blind date drove up in a red sports car that had seen better days, and so had he. Revving his car up to 35 miles an hour, we made it to his friend's apartment. There was no one there and the first thing my blind date did was close the blinds and lower the lights to set, as he said, the mood. Mood for what?

I said, "How about some music?"

"Let's make our own music," the man said.

I thought he wanted me to sing. That was not what he had in mind. When it became obvious that he had me on the bed in mind, I said, "I want to go home."

Reluctantly he took me home driving 25 miles an hour on the freeway.

My first real date was with a young man whom I met in a summer school English class at ELAC. Lorenzo Sandoval, Lonny for short, was extremely good looking, tall and dark and had been stationed in Japan when he was in the military. He is the one who renamed me Kay and it stuck. He worked as a Los Angeles police officer but aspired to become a dentist.

When my sponsor's wife asked me whom I was going out with and she heard the name, she said, "Oh, he's Mexican-American."

This is the first time I became personally aware that there were Americans and hyphenated Americans.

Lonny was Catholic and observed his religious customs and rituals. One day he came to pick me up in his policeman's uniform. I still had a thing about uniforms, having worn one for so long myself. But there was something wrong with Lonny's face. A smudge of dirt on his forehead. When I tried to wipe it away with a wet towel, he laughed.

"Let it be. My priest put it there. Don't you know that today is Ash Wednesday?"

"But it looks dirty."

"All the same, it shows that I was blessed."

I wondered how many more such rituals I would have to learn. If we were to get married, would our children have to follow those, too? These thoughts were in the back of my mind when we tried to talk seriously about our future. The other thing, not all the way in the back of my mind, was the fact that Lonny had other girl friends he went out with. I found out about one, Gloria, when Lonny took me to a Hollywood bar to celebrate my 21st birthday—my American coming of age and being allowed to drink in public.

"A gin and tonic, please" I said to the bartender.

"May I see your ID, please?" he replied.

"I don't have it with me, but it is my 21st birthday today."

"Sorry, ma'am!"

Lonny pulled out his police badge and assured the bartender that I told the truth.

"Sure. You want me to lose my license over this?"

It was a Shirley Temple for me.

On our way home, Lonny mentioned that he had been to the Hollywood Bowl the previous weekend.

"Alone?" I asked.

"No, I took Gloria," he replied.

"Is she your girlfriend?" I asked.

"Yeah, one of them," was his answer.

The concept of "playing the field," was new to me. I liked Lonny but I sensed expectations that I could not and would not want to meet. I was about to begin my college career, Lonny wanted to settle down and have a traditional family. After I made my decision that this would not work out, I found out later that he had married the 14-year-old daughter of his landlord.

My next serious boyfriend was Oliver Kilham, whose best friend's name was Goforth. Go-forth and Kill-em is how I memorized their names. Oliver had been married at 19 and divorced at 21. We met on an arranged blind date. Oliver was white and lived in the better part of Altadena with his well-to-do parents. Two older sisters were married with children. There was a younger brother, who wanted to be an "A" mechanic.

Both Oliver and I were then students in different colleges. We would see each other on weekends if he came home, and we corresponded on a regular basis. There were things about Oliver, attractive things, which made me feel that I had met a man more "substantial" than the ones I had dated before. Oliver was an outdoorsman. He introduced me to hiking and serious mountain climbing in the High Sierras. He, I, and three other men friends would climb up rocky mountains, and cross streams balancing on fallen trees. We camped in tents and cooked our own food, which we had carried on our backs with other survival necessities. I had never done anything like this, but was intensely proud to be able to keep up with four tough guys. Only when they decided to rope climb up a sheer cliff did I volunteer to stay behind and guard our belongings.

These mountain hiking tours were something oddly liberating for me. I felt like the whole world with all its problems was falling away from me. In a small literal, and large emotional, sense we were rising closer to the stars that blazed above us at night.

Oliver was also into expensive sports cars. When he came to pick me up in one of his prized possessions, a red Ferrari or black Alfa Romeo, I was the one to arrive at parties in a car all the other girls were dying to take a spin in. What made this all the more enticing was the fact that these cars were extremely low slung and passengers and driver had to kind of slide in. Naturally, a girl needed serious help from the handsome driver to get in and out of this machine.

Oliver had a touch of class I thought. That included nice restaurants and going to Shakespeare plays and classical concerts—things I liked to do but would usually not have done by myself. We had been seeing each other for a year when I was introduced to the rest of his family. The occasion was an Easter dinner get-together to which about a dozen family members were invited. As I watched Oliver's father stir a martini in a glass cylinder, I thought of some of the experiments in my chemistry lab in which foreign objects were dropped into a solution to see if they would dissolve. Some had done so, others had not. In this Easter dinner solution, I was going to be the foreign object.

When he was done with the mixing, father Kilham disappeared with his martini. Mother Kilham busied herself as if to avoid chatting. Oliver was talking to his siblings who would talk over and around me as if I did not exist. Later, at the table, I came to sit between the sisters who continued to talk to everyone across the table without ever saying a word to me. Oliver had mentioned that they were a close-knit family. Indeed, they were. All blond and blue-eyed and acres of fair skin among them.

Finally, the mother broke the ice and said apropos of nothing in particular, "Is your father a gardener? We have a Japanese gardener."

Continuing her monologue, she muttered, "Our family name is in the California Blue Book, you know."

For a moment I thought of books of Blue Chip Stamps, which could then still be exchanged for a broad range of consumer goods at redemption centers around the state.

Oliver noticed my puzzlement and difficulty to be properly impressed and explained, "It's like a 'Who's Who book."

"Big deal!" I thought.

My family name is in the history books and a whole Island bears our name. But I never was asked about my family and I did not volunteer any information. Instead, at the first chance, I quietly left the Kilham's home. When Oliver caught up with me, I was on the verge of tears. Yet, our relationship continued for a little while longer and Oliver even proposed marriage to me, engagement ring and all. He told me we would not have to live close to his family.

"But what about our children? They would not be blond and blue-eyed. In fact, their eyes would be dark, slanted and have Mongolian eyelids."

"The eyes can be fixed," Oliver said without thinking.

However, another problem had dogged our relationship all along—my hang-ups about sex. Preserving my virginity had been an article of faith with me and Oliver had honored this and had not pressured me to give in. Oliver eventually bought a house. Next door to his new domicile lived a young American girl, Betty, who took an immediate interest in her new neighbor. This young woman was not as constrained as I was. Whenever Oliver would return from one of our "hot" dates that had led nowhere in the lovemaking department, she would be waiting ready for him with home baked cookies to create a sweet mood. This arrangement did not clash with my Japanese moral standards, where a man keeping mistresses, and even second families, was socially acceptable, though not necessarily liked, by wives in such situations. To her credit, Oliver's attentive neighbor made no secret of their relationship. There was always evidence of her presence such as leaving her cosmetics and birth control pills for me to find. When Oliver and I decided to call it a day, Betty was grateful and overjoyed. In short order, they were married.

I had decided, and let it be known, that I would not get married before I had my B.A. degree. I was not entirely heartbroken when Oliver and I broke up for good. There was even some relief. Perhaps, I thought, my chance to play the field had arrived. I went out with different young men, though none of these dates developed into serious relationships. It did expand my social horizon somewhat. I attended a graduation prom with a Korean student at California State University at Los

Angeles (CSULA) that ended with him confessing at the end of the evening that he had a wife in Korea.

For fun, or so I thought, I filled out some forms that were passed around the school cafeteria by a computer dating service. In letters and phone calls, a number of interested males asked for my picture and other information.

The shortest phone call went like this, "How tall are you?"

"Five two."

"I like tall girls."

Click.

Others wrote me long letters, explaining their problems as well as likes and dislikes. I answered a few of the letters. The whole operation yielded one date—a very tall, very white man with shaven head who drove up in an open sports car. He took me to a deserted construction site up on a hill. There, he got out to pee, leaving me alone in the dark for an unexpectedly long while. When he returned, we sat in the open car and tried to have a conversation.

"I studied Einstein's Theory of Relativity and I can tell you where the fourth dimension is," he began.

Much later, when I was in another very single mode, I joined a video dating outfit that promised high success rates for an outrageous fee. I answered on video tape questions about my hobbies, my future goals and myself. Only two potential candidates contacted me. The first caller was German. We talked on the phone for an hour. He said I sounded like Connie Chung. We made a date, but he did not show up. The other was an Asian-Indian scientist. I refused. Before I turned down the Indian, whom I had not even met in person, there had been my date with Charlie Hope, who was from the Virgin Islands. Charlie had asked me to a dance at ELAC. He was a wonderful dancer and I liked him a lot. We had a wonderful evening until, at my door, he tried to kiss me good night. As his black face came close to mine, I withdrew instinctively. We were both surprised.

"It's the color, isn't it?"

"Well …"

When I was the president of the International Club at ELAC, I came in contact with students from many different countries and cultures. I got along with all of them and dated some. But I also discovered that when it came to being close with men "of color," I drew back. I had come up against one of the strongest cultural prejudicial taboos in my Japanese upbringing.

A more serious offer came my way from Larry Wong, an engineer at Hughes, who was considered the most eligible bachelor by his co-workers. At the first party we went to, he introduced me as his fiancée.

Larry lived well and made me a most attractive offer: "Study all you want, I'll pay for it. You'll have your own bank account."

This being at the time when I had to decide whether or not to go on to graduate school, I was tempted. Larry was romantic and gave me expensive presents with poems attached to them.

The most forceful proposal came from the most unexpected source, Lloyd Charles Wilson. Lloyd, "Mr. Wilson" to me up to then, was my sponsor and American "Papa." When I arrived and the Grubbs had delivered me to the Wilson's home, he and his wife had taken me in and under their wings like a daughter. In fact, they tried to adopt me, but were told that this could only happen with a child less than 14 years of age. No matter, from then on I called them Papa and Mama. The Wilsons loved me like their own child. They also spent money on me, as they would have for their own child. They fed and clothed me. They comforted me when I came up short against unfamiliar American customs. They corrected my English and taught me slang expressions. As I mentioned before, in their house I had my own room for the first time in my life. I observed and admired Mr. Wilson for his devotion to his handicapped wife. All of this changed the summer Mrs. Wilson went away for her course for the blind. I learned from both Wilsons that they were getting a divorce. I was sad about this, but they wanted to make clear that I was not the cause of their separation.

I had moved out of the house, but I stayed in contact with the divorced Wilsons. Mrs. Wilson moved back to live with her parents in Kansas. Mr. Wilson, now living in an apartment, was dating other women and introduced me to some of them. From time to time, we confided in each other and exchanged developments of which we were not necessarily very proud. In my case, it involved a passing liaison with a married man with a family. I was then 28 and people around me began to make the usual remarks about my still being single.

Giving up my home at the Wilsons had put me into a most precarious position as I have already described. Yet, the thought of chucking it all and going back to Japan never occurred to me. Before mantras were in, I had my own that I would repeat to myself when things looked dark, "*Gaman—Shimboo—nintai.*" They all mean endurance.

This is what my father had told me, "The harder you hit iron, the stronger it gets. The hardest part to build a railroad is to forge the rails."

One day, when Mr. Wilson and I were talking about our affairs and other difficulties, he asked me to marry him. He confessed that he had loved me all along and could not forget me even as he was dating and making love to other women. He said he loved me so much he could melt into his shoes.

"If you don't marry me, I'll kill myself," he said.

"I'll think about it."

And I did. Mr. Wilson, still Papa to me, was 20 years older than I was. He was physically in good shape and good looking. He was kind and a gentleman. I respected him as a teacher. He was not a stranger to me. I felt safe with him. He had protected me before. I felt an obligation to him for being my sponsor, my ticket to America, now perhaps, my transfer into permanent residency and American citizenship.

I wrote a letter to my parents informing them of my decision to marry Mr. Wilson. My father replied and said that he understood that it was a matter of *giri*. He knew how much I owed to Mr. Wilson. But my parents were not thrilled. They objected to the age difference. My future husband would be the same age as my stepmother. My stepmother was concerned about a family member with whom she could not communicate and whose culture was strange to her. In Japanese fashion, my parents maintained good manners, but could not bring themselves to give me their blessing. They did not encourage nor try to dissuade me, but they were also in no position to stop me. I had been back for visits. Each time my parents' hopes that a marriage with a Japanese suitor could be arranged, it had been dashed. The fiction that my stay in America was the passing phase of a headstrong daughter had long faded.

This was the summer when I had to decide where to go to graduate school. I wanted to do this, but I also had to because I was still living in the United States on a student visa, which required being enrolled as a full-time student. I also could not work legally more than 20 hours a week without a green card. On the day my visa was to expire, Mr. Wilson came to pick me up after class. I assumed that we were on our way to the immigration office, when he said, "You don't have to renew your visa. We'll go to city hall and get married instead."

Our wedding was a simple one. From the downtown Los Angeles City Hall, we went across the street into a small wedding chapel. The unplanned groom picked a street person from the sidewalk to function as our witness. Small change changed hands. Later, my American "sister," Chrystina Cook, a former classmate at ELAC and Cal State L.A., organized a real American style wedding. She loaned me her wedding gown and I fixed myself a veil. We invited some friends, including Oliver and the Wilson relatives, to the El Encanto Chapel in Monterey Park. This time I had a matron of honor and was led down the aisle by my husband's brother-in-law. No one from my family came to the wedding. There were no cards, telegrams or gifts.

After the ceremony, we rode off in our car festooned with a "JUST MARRIED" sign and old shoes and cans tied to the rear bumper. The guests threw rice at us. After a dinner at the Taix Restaurant in Echo Park, we checked into the Statler Hilton Hotel in downtown Los Angeles. Lloyd, as Papa now wanted me to call him, had had too much to drink to drive his new bride to Palm Springs for our honeymoon. When we got there the next day, our reservation for our suite had been canceled, and we wound up in a dingy motel in a room with two twin beds.

We spent a few days roaming around Palm Springs, took the tram up Mount San Jacinto, and hiked around some. I was resting by a little stream by myself when I realized fully and for the first time that I WAS MARRIED. I should now be happy and contented, elated and excited. I was none of these. Still, I thought I must have done something right because my husband appeared to be extremely happy.

One practical advantage of being married to an American citizen was that I now could proceed with my studies at my own pace, or not proceed at all. I took one semester off, then did one year of student teaching at Montebello and Mark Keppel high schools, before getting a secondary teaching credential. In my spare time, I taught at Berlitz language school and did private tutoring in Japanese.

One of my private students was a local family doctor. When my husband went there to get an EKG done, the nurse accused him of fondling her.

"We are filing charges of indecent behavior against your husband," the nurse's lawyer barked at me over the phone.

"I will counter sue you for libel. My husband has been teaching with an unblemished record for more than 20 years. You tell your nurse we will sue her, too."

Within minutes, the lawyer called back, "We are dropping the charges."

We had been married for three months. I was mad at the nurse and the doctor. I was mad at myself for being unable to suppress doubt about my husband, who, about that time, began drinking and smoking heavily. This was a side of the former Mr. Wilson I had never experienced in the years I was living as "the daughter" in his household. Without being fully aware of it at first, I began to create my own world, a world in which I was very busy almost all the time.

I've already mentioned my stint at teaching Japanese at Berlitz. On my first day there the director came in and asked me if I wanted to teach the Monkees.

"At which zoo would that be?"

I had never heard of this group of rock musicians before. We drove to the Screen Gem Studio in Hollywood where I met the famous TV stars of "Here Come the Monkees."

I was to teach all four of them phrases like, "Hi, I'm Peter Tork, I'm Ricky Dolenz, I'm David Jones, I'm Michael Nesmith. We love Japan and the Japanese, thank you and good bye."

The Monkees were recording a new album, The Royal Flush. I coached them individually between takes. In our cubicle a red light blinking meant a call to the studio. We kept an eye on that light while rehearsing some very basic Japanese. Peter Tork was more serious and signed up for extra language lessons on Saturday afternoons. He invited me to his house in the Hollywood

Hills. I met his companion and toddler son and had my first all-natural-foods lunch.

The word got around to a local newspaper in Alhambra. They sent a staff writer and photographer.

"Are you union members?" the cameraman on the set asked them.

"No."

"Sorry, you can't work here, but your reporter can."

I was interviewed and the cameraman took pictures of Peter Tolk with me posing in a Kimono and a stuffed monkey in the middle. A former friend from PL leaked the information of our arrival in Japan. We were met by a chauffeured limousine from Myoojo, a major weekly magazine, and taken directly to an expensive restaurant in Akasaka, the famous former red light district of Tokyo. While my husband ate his first authentic Japanese meal with chopsticks, *Sashimi* and all, I was being interviewed with flashlights blazing. This being an "exclusive," the chauffeur stayed with us for security reasons. This is how we were taken to my brother's home in Tateyama, south of Tokyo. The exclusive did not hold for long. No sooner had we arrived at my brother's place than reporters from other magazines had gathered at the door and were clamoring for my attention. My sister-in-law went to answer the door, but was at a total loss as to what to say. Politeness towards strangers, the only thing she knew, would not do.

My fifteen minutes of fame actually lasted longer and I learned all over again how "small" Japan is in more ways than one. A weekly magazine featuring an article about my teaching the Monkees made the rounds across the country. In Osaka, my mother rushed out to buy a stack of that special issue and was distributing copies to all family members along with the Monkees' autographed photographs. Wherever we visited family, we were treated like stars.

In Hokkaido a group of crazed teenage fans mobbed us as we were coming out of the airport and one of them shouted, "I want to slash you with a razor blade!"

From then on I wore sunglasses and a scarf over my head.

Our trip to Japan was to introduce my husband to my family. That part appeared to be going exceedingly well. Everywhere we went my relatives rose to heights of hospitality. Those we had not been to, as yet, would call the ones we had visited already to find out what they had cooked for us so that they would not bore us with a repetition. My brother, who speaks very limited English, discovered common interests with my husband involving mostly smoking and alcohol. Communication was, of course, a problem, as most of my Japanese relatives know no

English and Lloyd spoke no Japanese. Gestures and sign language were important. Occasionally, this led to funny and startling encounters. One example was how my step-grandmother attempted to tell my husband to relax and cool off on a very hot day. Wearing nothing but a simple cotton *yukata*, she opened the front to wave the sides for air. My husband got the message, but did not respond in kind. Generally, all seemed sweetness and light and I was surprised and touched.

Only later, after our divorce, did I learn the true reason my family had acted in such an exemplary manner. My step-grandmother had told her daughters, my aunts, "You must be extremely nice to them, because this is a case of *nasanu naka.*" This meant she was not the blood-related daughter of mother Masako. None of my stepmother's relatives are my blood relatives.

In Japanese culture, this "handicap" is overcome by extreme politeness and hospitality. My aunts obediently followed their mother's advice. All had had their reservations, which they exchanged amongst themselves, but kept from me.

15

Either She Moves Out Or I Will

One day a moving van pulled up in our driveway. My mother-in-law climbed down from the passenger seat and began giving directions to the movers.

When I opened the door, Katharine Wilson, whom I had never met before, said with a big smile, "Well, here I am! I'm Lloyd's mother. I'm retired and I have come to live with my son."

With this, she looked around the house to see where her furniture would go. I watched in secret horror as a piano replaced our stereo and TV set. Our furniture was mostly second hand and plenty used. Katharine claimed hers was mostly antiques. We were being upgraded and getting a good deal.

"How long are you going to stay with us?" I asked.

She smiled. "Why, I already told you, I've come to live with my son."

When Lloyd came home later and I confronted him, he said, "Now, now, we can decide these things later. Can't you offer my mother something to drink?"

I quickly went to the kitchen and prepared my best Japanese green tea.

"Oh, I don't drink green tea; I'd rather have a cup of coffee."

Not a big matter, but already I could have thrown the teapot at her. My husband avoided the subject.

I was back in school working on a master's degree in Asian Studies at USC and teaching part-time. I spent relatively little time at home. But when I was there, I deeply resented my mother-in-law's telling me what to do and not to do.

"The toilet paper rolls out the wrong way. You should always cook pork well or we'll all get trichinosis. What are the ingredients of these dumplings?"

Sometimes I turned off the gas and went to my bedroom.

One day I gave Lloyd an ultimatum, "Either she moves out or I will."

She did. We still lived in walking distance of each other but this improved our relationship. Katharine would come to visit often to play scrabble. That was difficult for me. I had to look up many words and was at a disadvantage when words were argued about.

One night, my husband had a mild heart attack at four in the morning. It was mild enough for him to refuse an ambulance. I drove him to the ER at White Memorial Hospital, where he was kept for observation for a week. I drove my mother-in-law for a visit. On our way there, she drove me crazy telling me how to drive. Once there, she spilled hot coffee on her son in her efforts to tell him what and how to eat his hospital food.

"Get out of here!" he shouted.

We left in a hurry.

Three months later, our lives were back to normal. I now had my M.A. from USC behind me, had secured the full-time position at UC Irvine, but was also still teaching part-time at Pasadena City College in the evening. It was a full schedule leaving little time and energy for running a household and catering to the expectations of a husband and his mother. Usually, I would leave my husband sitting already half drunk at the dinner table, before rushing off to my evening classes. Leftovers and dirty dishes awaited when I came home.

One evening on my way to Pasadena, a driver high on drugs who raced through a red light on Huntington Drive hit me. When I came to, a man in a white coat was leaning over me. There is a Japanese superstition that when you are about to die, a man in white will help you cross the river that separates this world from the other world. I tried to refuse this man's help. I was not ready to cross the river, as yet. When he tried to move me, I felt a terrible pain. I was still alive. Tears ran down my face, but I was smiling.

I heard the paramedic speak into his microphone: "... multiple bone fractures ... possible brain damage ..."

We now had a heart attack and serious car accident between us. But we also had scheduled an extensive trip through Europe; tickets booked and fully paid a year in advance without possibility of a refund. My husband checked me out of the hospital the night of the accident with my right arm immobilized in a sling and my collar, shoulder and wrist bones fractured, not to mention multiple bruises and contusions all over my body. At home, a kitchen full of unwashed dishes.

There were other surprises. Without telling me, my husband had put our house up for sale. The day after I returned from the hospital he packed up his gear and went fishing. I answered the door in my hospital gown to show the house to prospective buyers. I took the first offer, to the chagrin of agents who thought they had better offers from their clients. I have no idea where my husband found the motley crew of characters who appeared on our doorsteps on moving day. They looked like extras from a third-rate comedy movie or cartoon. They moved the large pieces. I packed the rest with my left hand.

Summer came too soon for me to be fully healed or have the use of my right arm back. I was apprehensive about going on a ten-week trip of Europe, covering 13 countries. My husband had let himself be guided by Frommer's "Europe on $5 to $10 a day." This was not my idea of "doing" all the famous places I had heard and dreamed about. My romantic notion of visiting Paris, for example, included sitting in an outdoor café on the

Champs Elysée, watching chic Parisiennes stroll by while I sip a glass of fine wine. My husband reasoned that the price of one glass of wine on the Champs Elysée would buy a whole bottle of the same wine in an out of the way bar with a pinball machine thrown in. He had all the cheap places to eat underlined in his guidebook. When I was thinking of escargot on the *rive gauche*, he was thinking of soup and bread with the railroad workers near the tracks. This is how we made our way by tour bus and trains across the continent.

We had to plan for our hotels as we went along. Wherever we arrived for the night I would stay at the station with the luggage, while my husband walked as far as his weakened heart would allow to find a cheap place to sleep. Elevators, air-conditioning and porters in the lobby were warning signs for places to be avoided. I, being the one-armed porter, sent two of our suitcases home and we continued like poor students on an endless hike. Not long into the trip we were hardly talking to each other. On the bus or train, we did not sit next to each other. But all our money was in traveler's checks signed by him. This was before credit cards became the common and international currency.

With my background in studying art, I concentrated on museums. I visited practically all the famous ones and much of the art I had studied I now saw in original form. My husband spent his time on different pursuits, which included, to my consternation, a tour of the Paris sewers.

It is sometimes suggested that traveling together is a good way to test a relationship. We failed this test. Shortly after our return we had a kind of debriefing.

"I really did not enjoy this trip."

"You are ungrateful."

"I want a divorce."

"I'm a sick man, you have to take care of me; you owe it to me."

This went on for some time with my husband vacillating between heaping verbal abuse on me and begging me to stay with him. A friend told me about a one room apartment in Newport Beach close to UC Irvine. One day I packed as much as I could carry and moved there. My husband made attempts at reconciliation. Eventually, he agreed to a divorce under one condition—I was not to ask for any property or support. I agreed under the condition that he would leave me alone and make no claims against me. Six months later the divorce became final. But this was not the end, as yet. My now ex-husband would call and leave messages.

"I'm lonely. I want you back!"

I erased his messages. One day he was waiting at my door. I hesitated. I smelled alcohol on his breath.

"What do you want? It's finished. It's all over with us."

"Can we talk inside?" he said, as he pushed himself and me through the door.

He looked around my sparsely furnished apartment. There was a ceiling lamp sitting on the floor.

"Nice lamp," he said.

We sat and talked for a while. There was little to talk about. It became clear that he had not come only to talk. When it was over, he put on his clothes and, as he was walking towards the door, picked up the lamp and left. I moved to another apartment and told everyone not to reveal my new address. However, one evening as I was having dinner alone, he showed up again.

"I miss your cooking," he said.

I tried to stall. "I have only one piece of meat."

"Half will do," he countered

He told me that his girlfriend, a divorcée who played golf with him, had just gone back to her former husband. Why could we not do the same thing?

"I'm perfectly happy."

"Well, just remember that I asked you."

This time, he carried away a small bookcase as he left.

I said quietly, "If you ever show up again, I'll call the police."

That was the last time I saw him.

16

Daughter Of A Gun

♦

Teppoo Musume

For many people divorce is traumatic, financially ruinous and emotionally shattering. With me, it was the opposite on all accounts. I had left a mismatch, had gotten a messy situation under control, and began to be financially independent. Emotionally, being single in midlife was another matter. I instinctively threw myself into work and compensatory activities. There were three major events that changed my life for the better. I got a full-time teaching position at ELAC, my Alma Mater where I had started as a foreign student. On the strength of this and before I had tenure, I scraped together enough money for a down payment on a large townhouse in Monterey Park. For the first time in my life I owned my own home. I applied for U.S. citizenship and in due time was sworn in at the Ahmanson Theater in Los Angeles with thousands of others.

Before this all came to pass, I still lived in my one room apartment in Newport Beach, where my parents came to visit with hopes of taking me back to Japan. As I said before, for a number of years I had maintained the fiction for the benefit of my family that my stay in the United States was temporary and that I would eventually return home. This had worn thin when I got married. Now, after my divorce, my parents' hopes were raised once again. To them my coming home seemed to be the better part of wisdom. I had lost a husband and my job at UC Irvine. When they arrived, I was drawing unemployment compensation.

To my parents' and my surprise, I contrived to take us on a grand tour of the American West paying for it with money refunded from my retirement plan and leftover money from an accident settlement. My parents went home without me. Reluctantly they agreed that I was truly a *teppoo musume,* a bullet that once it leaves the barrel of a gun will never return.

My parents came to visit me again when my circumstances had improved. This time they joined me in a two bedroom apartment, already quite upscale by Japanese standards considering that I was a single woman. But the real shock came when they visited me for a third time, for what turned out to be my father's last trip. Now I was living in a two story, three bedroom townhouse that I owned outright. In Japan, it would be considered all but immoral for one single woman to occupy so much space all by herself. In fact, Japanese real estate agents would strongly discourage such a sale. My townhouse could accommodate two families—the parents with their children and children's children. I was aware of this luxury, every time I put the key into my front door. I rose to modest heights as an interior decorator and enjoyed the results immensely. In my handkerchief garden, I planted vegetables, flowers, and trees.

Again, I took my parents on an even grander tour through four states. I did most of the driving with my sister at my side and my parents fast asleep in the back seat. Once, my sister offered to drive. No sooner had she taken the wheel, than my father awoke.

He saw who was driving and said, "I cannot die yet, I haven't seen the Grand Canyon."

My sister and I switched positions. It had been one of my father's wishes to see the Grand Canyon before he died.

He stood there for a long time taking in the panoramic view, then turned and said, "Now I can die anytime."

"But I have so much more to show you."

"You cannot be greedy. Many of my friends are waiting for me on the other side."

Later, as my father was taken onto the plane in a wheelchair, he thanked me for fulfilling his last wish and said, "This is our final good-bye."

One morning three months later, when I was leaving for work and was already outside my door, I heard the phone ringing. Normally, I would have ignored it and let the answering machine take the message. This morning I went back inside and picked up the receiver.

"Hallo, big sister, I just want you to know that father has died. Big brother told me, 'don't bother to call, she can't make it in time anyway,' but I thought you should know."

"When is the funeral?" I asked.

"Day after tomorrow. We are having a wake right now."

"I'll be at the funeral."

I rushed to my office and handed a week's worth of lesson plans to my department chair. I called my travel agent who informed me that the only ticket he could get on such short notice was for first class with Japan Airlines—the most expensive one covering this route. Once on the plane and now traveling in luxury, I tried my best to calm my nerves by downing one free cup of *sake* after another. I should have been totally drunk by the time the plane landed at Narita airport, but I was not.

When I arrived at the funeral parlor, my family and a large crowd of mourners dressed in black and white were already gathered inside and many more were standing outside. My father's casket with the lid already closed rested at the center of a large altar. Since I had missed *okuri-mizu,* the final sendoff water ritual, the casket was opened once more only for me. I was given a pair of chopsticks and a bowl with a small cotton ball soaked in water. I picked up the cotton ball and cleansed my father's mouth.

My father looked very peaceful, almost smiling as if he were saying, "Oh, you made it to my funeral!"

I took his hand in mine. It was cold but soft. At that moment, my father's simple gold wedding band came off his right middle finger and dropped onto the palm of my hand.

Those around me said in unison, "Your father wanted you to have it. We tried, but could not remove it before."

I have been wearing this ring on my right middle finger, like my father used to wear it, ever since.

My father's body was cremated according to Buddhist custom. All but the bones of a body are burned. When this was completed, my father's bones were returned to us and my brother, the veterinarian, began showing off his anatomical knowledge by explaining and pointing out the different bones of the skeleton. All of a sudden a rage, like at my mother's funeral when I was a child, came over me. This was my father now reduced to white bones being lectured over by my brother. I tried to hide myself away but was called back. I was handed a set of unmatched chopsticks to pick "my" bone and place it into the funeral urn. Everyone in my immediate family followed my example. Then my brother placed a bone he called "Buddha's throat" on top. The funeral urn is kept at home for forty-nine days. That is how long the soul will remain there, too. Then the urn, with a tablet engraved with the name of the deceased, is moved to its final resting place in a small tomb or mausoleum.

In Japan when someone dies, it is customary for family and friends to send the widow or widower money called *koden* (incense money) in lieu of flowers. Impeccable records of the donors' names and the amounts of money are kept so that appropriate gifts of appreciation can be mailed out promptly.

When we return home from the funeral, someone has to throw a pinch of salt over our shoulder before we enter the house. That will ward off evil spirits and keep them from entering the house with us. This is not the end of the prescribed rituals. Now come the visits to the widow's or widower's neighbors formally notifying them of what has happened and asking for their indulgence and help. In our case, the former husband of my deceased older sister and I were chosen for this awkward duty. From door to door we went, bowing and mumbling our pleas like incantations in church. My stepmother appreciated our efforts, but I felt only relief when it was over and I was home again in America.

17

To My Roots

I had hoped to make a trip to my roots in China with my father. We had talked about it many times until it was too late. Now I joined a group on a tour to Hong Kong and part of mainland China. A part-time Chinese instructor at ELAC who had told me that he needed an aide led the tour. He got a free trip out of this—I did not. I helped out and led the group when our guide was otherwise engaged. In fact, he did become engaged and married a young Chinese woman, a graduate from Beijing University ten years older than his daughter, while we were there.

In Beijing I left the group for a day to trace where my family had been living. I carried my birth certificate that showed the address of the house in which I had been born. A Japanese friend of my brother's in Beijing was to help me find the house. I called Mr. Yokoyama from the lobby of my hotel to make arrangements to meet him. The hotel receptionist overheard our conversation and spoke to me in Japanese. He said he lived in the neighborhood where we used to live. Tomorrow was his day off. He invited both Mr. Yokoyama and me for lunch at his house. A taxi took us to a tiny house where this receptionist lived with his wife, and his brother and his wife. With pride, our hosts gave us a tour of the house that featured a refrigerator and TV in the living room, and a bathtub behind a curtain close to the entrance of the kitchen where the wives were preparing homemade dumplings. There was also an outhouse in front of the house. After a very nice lunch, we walked around the neighborhood. Before we left, our host had explained that he would walk behind us because he was not allowed to have close contacts with foreigners. Inviting us was risky already, but his dream was to study in Japan and he hoped that we could help him.

At the local police station, we asked for directions. When I showed my birth certificate, the man in charge pointed to where we should go. We meandered around narrow streets in an area that had not been razed, as yet, for the horrendous, container-like new high-rise apartment blocks beginning to ring the cities. When we came to what I thought was "our" house I took pictures. The large house with an interior courtyard was now subdivided into many individual units, all padlocked. There was no way to go inside. I had expected that a visit to my birthplace would be one of the high points of my journey. Now, standing in front of this house looking and taking pictures, triggered no memories. When I sent the pictures to my brother, who had done his own roots thing before me, I learned that I had been to the wrong house, but one that had the same address as the right one. My brother had actually talked to the new occupants, who confirmed his memory of a leak in the ceiling and told him that the leak was still working.

Travel in Communist China in the late 1980's had its challenges. For one, you had to stay with the group. That was the safe thing to do in a country whose language you did not speak, but it was also required by the Chinese authorities. If you planned separate excursions, you needed a special permit. To get one was a bureaucratic nightmare. This was contrary to advice from our travel agent in Monterey Park who said everything could be arranged in Beijing. When I went to apply for a one-week extension to travel on my own a stoic policeman stared at my passport without looking at or speaking to me. After minutes of silence, still not looking at me, he abruptly handed me back the passport without saying a word.

As we made our way across China by train and bus, we were impressed by the well-known historical sites. But what really touched me was the sense of tremendous energy of a people in transition. This was no longer the locked-down Communist-planned economy. Signs of budding free enterprise were everywhere, starting with the private vendors surrounding us wherever we stopped. We stopped often because there was so much building going on that traffic holdups were common. I had seen the endless crowds of bicyclists on TV. But it is a different experience to see it all up close on streets that one might want to cross and cannot. Our visit was shortly before the Democracy Movement. I cannot say whether there was a sense of hope in the air but a lightening of the atmosphere had occurred. Where before almost the entire population wore minor variations of the Mao outfit, a severe uniform of khaki pants and jacket in the summer, quilted upright sleeping bags in the winter, people were now sporting colorful shirts and blouses and Western suits and dresses.

Left over from stricter Communist days was the separation of foreigners from local residents by providing different currencies for the two. With their special currency, foreigners could buy luxury items in special department stores where local residents could look but were not able to buy with their money. It made only good economic sense, therefore, for enterprising Chinese merchants and vendors to demand our money for their goods. For us it meant that all the local Chinese currency we had exchanged for our money was worthless.

One private enterprise that seemed to be flourishing was magic. Not the conventional kind where the viewers may lose their wristwatches and wallets but get them back at the end of the show. This magic was the kind where the loss of valuables is permanent. I was lucky, but some of my fellow travelers were not.

Ours was not what is known in the travel industry as a top of the line tour. We generally carried our luggage ourselves. Suitcases on rollers did not take well to unpaved, often sticky roads and walkways. If we had help, it was worse. Our luggage was then simply thrown out of the windows of the trains. This is how my precious bottle of Johnny Walker's whiskey came to soak my clothes.

The Chinese have a reputation for being able to eat everything. This must be how they develop immunity to germs that would do strangers in. To avoid this fate meant no fresh fruit and vegetables anywhere throughout our trip with the exception of Hong Kong. We were also cautioned to be very careful not to drink tap water or colored soft drinks sold on the street. In the frightful heat, we bought what looked like sealed bottles of warm water. In one place, a woman was following us around collecting empty bottles. I saw her take them to a stand where a man refilled them from an open pitcher, before putting on caps to re-sell them as new. I gave the woman my unopened bottle. She thanked and thanked me.

In addition to returning to my birthplace, I had planned this trip to include other Asian countries of which I teach the history and cultures in my courses. After leaving my tour group in Hong Kong, my next stop on my own was Taiwan. In China, our tour guides had explained to us that many sites they were showing us had been national treasures plundered by the

Chiang Kai-Shek regime when it fled the mainland for the Island of Formosa. Now, as I toured the National Palace Museum in Taipei, the guide explained that they had so many art objects that they could put on completely new shows every three months. As I came upon the priceless collections of Jade carvings, I could not help but wonder if some of the items displayed might have been part of my father's possessions, which the Chinese government officials had confiscated at the end of the war.

I visited Toroko Gorge to take slides, which I would use for a number of years to show in my classes. Toroko Gorge was and is a setting for many movies. The gorge created by a river provides panoramic vistas that are breathtaking. It also yields an abundance of marble that is used to carve statues and millions of tourist souvenirs.

Taiwan has an aboriginal population that is not well known. These native Taiwanese live in the eastern part of the island, called *Hoaren*. Upon my arrival by plane, a bus brought me to a village where Aborigines in bright, colorful costumes and headdress sang and danced to entertain the tourists. Song and dance were participatory and, before I knew it, I was singing and dancing with the natives. The dance involved sudden turns that threw me up against some of the other dancers who were dancing barefoot, while I was in tennis shoes. After I stepped on a number of bare feet, they were happy to let me quit. These native rituals are said and meant to be spiritual. But like the American Indian pow-wows I had taken part in once before, I was not spiritually moved. I was so obviously a tourist for whom the local residents put on a show to make a living. At the end, I was offered photographs of myself dancing.

On my next stop in Seoul, South Korea, I arrived in the middle of preparations for the upcoming Olympic Games. To make a good impression on the rest of the world involved a huge effort of the whole population. I was not interested in that. I wanted to see and get a feel of what it meant to be living in a divided country, a fate South Korea then still shared with Germany. Friends drove me to the demilitarized zone, or DMZ, a swath of land fortified on both sides by walls and fences topped by barbed wire, broken by guard towers at certain intervals. As we approached, we came upon a large memorial tower where South Korean people come to make offerings of food and flowers in memory of relatives who had died in North Korea or while trying to flee south. Not far from this tower sat a train stopped in its tracks, so to speak, on its way from Seoul to Pyong Yang. Of all the images in this divided country, this train going nowhere moved me the most. My Korean friends put it this way, "*Kasma puge,*" my heartaches, the title of a Korea song popular in Japan.

There came a point beyond which my South Korean friends were not allowed to go. Two of the guards who were American

GI's took me in tow. Together we marched up to the fence. What I could see on the other side without binoculars were soldiers who looked very Korean to me. The same went for the scenery in general. Rice fields on "our" side, rice fields on "their" side. A strange atmosphere prevailed. As I stood there with the American soldiers around me, no one spoke a word. Like in a church, it did not occur to me to ask questions.

As my South Korean friends were driving me around, they talked about what life had been like during 35 years of Japanese occupation. It had divided Koreans into those who were pro and those who were anti-Japanese. Dividing lines often ran through families and friendships. Koreans who adopted Japanese ways and culture spoke Japanese and might even send their children to Japan to study. They dressed in Kimono for special occasions and lived in Japanese style houses with *tatami* floors instead of Korean *ondol*, floors that could be heated with steam diverted from the kitchen. The pro-Japanese fared well under the Japanese regime. They harbored fewer resentments or hatred toward Japanese after the occupiers had left.

The opposite was true for the anti-Japanese Koreans. Many fled the country to China, Russia and America. Together with Koreans who stayed, they organized anti-Japanese movements and lobbied for Korean independence. Those Koreans ran secret schools to teach the Korean language and culture which the Japanese occupation authorities had forbidden. My friends were, of course, pro-Japanese, but at least one of them reminisced about members of his family who had been on the "other" side.

My last stop on this trip was Japan. There is always a moment of recognition when I come off the plane at Narita airport and suddenly everyone around me speaks Japanese. I become part of the crowd of people rushing from here to there, all giving the impression that they know exactly where they are going. I, too, know where I am going and can ask questions and give answers and orders in a familiar language.

18

Where Is Your Uncle?

After my divorce, I changed my name back to Tanegashima. I reconnected with some of my old friends. I invited my family to come and visit from Japan. Should the topic of a possible remarriage come up, as it often did, I told all those, who didn't really want to listen, that my life as a single woman was just fine. In a way it was. I was free in my decisions in what I wanted and did not want to do, in whom I wanted and did not want to see, where I wanted or did not want to go. I was alone, but not lonely. Or so I thought until that first New Year's Eve all by myself. As the crackle of fireworks erupted all around me, I started to cry. I opened my window, raised my *sake* cup and called out into the darkness, "HAPPY NEW YEAR!" I had never been so lonesome in all my life.

My evenings were mostly taken up teaching night classes. Often I dreaded another three-hour evening class after a day of teaching, only to find that I came away from those classes invigorated and happy. Evening students tend to be older, more mature and more interested in what they are studying. One such student was John Hayden, one of my older and better students. In the following semester, one of my new younger students, Bill, blushing deeply, mentioned that his uncle John had recommended my course. Bill, who would later be one of the engineers working on NASA's JPL Mars exploration, was extremely shy. He sat in the last row and helped me with the movie projector. He offered to escort me to my car. On those short walks, I learned more about his family and he explained that this uncle of his was really a close family friend, renting living quarters in his parent's house. I also learned that this student in his early 20's was a loner without a girlfriend, but intensely interested in finding one. When the semester was over, we agreed to stay in touch, something easily said and seldom done. Not so with Bill. When his uncle suggested that we all see a Kurosawa movie together, I readily agreed and suggested that we have dinner together beforehand. Bill showed up alone.

"Where's your uncle?"

"He couldn't make it. Something came up."

"Does he want me to be your girlfriend?" I said jokingly.

"Yes," Bill said simply, blushing in what I now thought was such a charming way.

We kept our relationship secret for a while. But one day Bill insisted that I meet his family. It was with some trepidation that I, the older woman and his former teacher, went along.

As we walked into the house, Bill announced, "I now have a girlfriend, her name is Kaori Tanegashima."

"Hallelujah!" cried Uncle John.

Father Fred, mother Suzanne and sister Laura went on as though this was the most normal thing to happen and I quickly became part of the family. Friday dinners were at the Caramba, a Mexican restaurant in Alhambra. The idea was to relax and unwind with a margarita before the food arrived. We brought each other up to date on the week's happenings, and Fred and John had their chance to air their deep resentment, not to say hatred, of lawyers and politicians.

On that subject, at first, I mostly listened. In fact, when the two men got hot under their collars, I realized that up to this point I had hardly been interested in politics. I had tried to keep up with the history, statistics and current developments in Japan because I was often asked questions by people who assumed that I was an expert in those matters. But politics was a topic of mostly heated discussions in Bill's family. I wanted to be part of these stimulating matches. With the whole family free-for-all, it was difficult to get a word in. They were all well up on American history, and I learned a lot. When the subject came around to Japan or Japanese in America, I got my moments of attention.

Bill and his family took sports seriously and watched football and basketball games religiously. Although I had been into competitive sports myself as a teenager, until I met Bill I had never had an interest in big league American sports. Now, part of our lives had to be arranged around important games. While Bill watched the Lakers or the Rams, I would grade papers or write letters. I sometimes explain this in my classes as an example of cross-cultural tolerance.

Bill had an apartment. I had bought my townhouse. Moving in together would have made good sense. Bill was all for it. I hesitated. After a marriage with a much older man gone bad, I had serious reservations about a long-term commitment with a much younger man. Bill never asked if I had been married before. I did not volunteer to tell him that I was closer to his parent's age than his own. He said age difference did not matter to him. It did to me. I did not want children. He did. I encouraged Bill to see other girls, and he did. We developed what amounted to an open relationship. When he told me that he was living with a Chinese girl, I accepted it. When I got engaged to Joel, Bill had mixed emotions. There was a long pause on the phone.

"What is it, Bill?" I asked. "Aren't you going to congratulate me?"

"Can I come over to see you?"

We had a most proper last date, "Would we, could we stay friends?"

When I told Joel about Bill and his family, the first thing he said was, "There is no reason why we shouldn't all stay friends."

We danced at each other's weddings and have remained close.

19

Everything You Have Been Wishing For …

On one of my visits to Japan for a New Year's family get together, my father gave each of his children and grandchildren a *Haiku* in beautiful Japanese calligraphy on narrow *shikishi* paper. For me he had written:

Omoiishi,	Everything you have been wishing
koto mina narite,	has come true and now you can
Chiyo no haru.	celebrate the thousand years' spring

"But father," I protested, "I still have not found a good husband."

"You will find one soon," my father said with quiet authority. Soon would take some time fifteen years to be exact.

I am often asked if I could or would ever want to go "home" to Japan to live there when I am old and alone. Many immigrants to the United States from all parts of the world have done this, and many are still doing or planning to do it. I have no such plans. For me, coming to America and being able to make a life for myself was my life's defining experience. It was and continues to be liberating in such a fundamental way that I could not imagine fitting myself back into the confinements of Japanese society. To come "home," now means to come back to America. It also means coming back to a new life with a new husband.

I had known Joel for a number of years. He taught political science in the social science department where I had become a member. Joel almost never attended department meetings or social gatherings. He taught his classes from 9 to 12 in the morning and was gone the moment his last class ended. The reason for this was a wife suffering from MS and needing constant care.

From time to time, we might pass each other in the hallways. He would compliment me on my wardrobe.

One of his not totally original lines was, "You look like you just stepped out of VOGUE."

Of course, I did not mind hearing him say so. Only once, at a colleague's trailer home, I caught a glance of Joel's wife in a wheelchair as they were leaving.

"What a devoted husband," I thought.

Ten years had gone by, when our department chair came around collecting signatures for a sympathy card after Joel's wife had died. The thought crossed my mind that he was now available. But even though he was now free, his participation in campus activities did not increase much. We saw no more of each other than all the years before.

It was the last day before Christmas vacation. I was going around our office distributing Christmas cards. Joel sat at his desk. I wished him Merry Christmas.

As I was handing him his card I said, "Do you have plans for Christmas vacation?"

"No, nothing special, do you?"

"No, nothing special."

He said no more. I went back to my office wondering what was the matter with this guy. I provide a perfect opening and NOTHING. I went back to find out.

"If you are not doing anything special and I am not doing anything special, maybe we could do nothing special together?"

"YES!"

"Your neck of the woods or mine?"

"Yours."

"You want me to show you Little Tokyo?"

"Fine."

I made a reservation at the Thousand Cranes restaurant at the New Otani Hotel. The restaurant at the third floor level looks onto a Japanese garden with a pond, trees, rocks and waterfall. It is a favorite spot for weddings. Since both of us were early, that is where we sat and talked until the restaurant opened. We talked as though we had known each other well for a long time.

Joel had his first authentic Japanese meal and discovered that he could use chopsticks naturally and deftly. Later we toured Little Tokyo. I bought him a black T-shirt with a crane that became one of his favorites and still is. The crane is the symbol of longevity and peace. To be on the safe side, I bought one for myself, too.

We browsed through the Little Tokyo bookstore and I checked our animal zodiac signs in a Japanese almanac. Ours, Bird and Rabbit the book said, were the worst combination for a marriage. In jest, Joel wiped his brow. We went to my house and talked and talked. There was much ground to cover. We had much in common. There was the superficial stuff, like Danish furniture, type of music, neatness and attention to aesthetics in the home. Our lives showed more serious parallels, also. We had similar defining war and postwar experiences that had formed some of our attitudes and perspective on life. We both came to the United States at different times, but both at 19 years of age. We both knew that coming to America was final and that we would become U.S. citizens and live the rest of our lives here. We had adapted well and become Americans without giving up or denying our Japanese and German cultural heritage. We both liked Los Angeles and we liked being teachers. On my imaginary checklist a mess of buttons began to light up.

Age: perfect.

Intelligence/education: high.

Financial: comfortable.

Personality: high energy, kind, gentle, reliable, neat, good taste, even-tempered, open-minded and considerate.

Interests: Similar and common in music, art, furniture and much more.

Looks: Not objectionable.

Physique: Slim/trim. Excellent health.

Habits: Non-smoker, non-alcoholic, good manners, no nail chewing, nose picking, ass tickling and ball scratching in public.

Sense of humor: Witty, spontaneous, he makes me laugh.

Profession: Same as mine. Many common points of reference, same work schedule.

Residence: Home in Pacific Palisades.

Family: His mother and two of his siblings have been divorced, but all remained close friends.

Was this too good to be true? Could this be real? Was this the man I had been waiting for?

"Would you like to stay for dinner?"

"I'd better be going," he mumbled.

"Ok," I said, "you don't have to call me, we'll just get together whenever, no strings attached …"

Later, Joel told me that as he was putting on his shoes before leaving, he thought to himself, "If I were not such a complete idiot, I would ask her if I should stay not only for dinner but for the night."

He did not stay, but called me as soon as he got home to tell me that he missed me.

To be open and up front, not to mention modern and emancipated, I asked, "What kind of relationship do you have in mind, sexual or asexual?"

"An asexual relationship I can have with my dog," he answered.

Either way would have been all right with me. I wanted the companionship, a friend to talk to, a man to be comfortable with.

For our next date, I cooked a *tempura* dinner. Joel arrived with one rose in one hand and his robe over one arm. He had hoped, he told me later, that the symbolism wouldn't be too hard to divine. It was not. The dinner went well. More talk. And then it was time for a little *Sake* and *Ofuro* in my deep steel bath tub imported from Japan. In it one soaks in very hot water up to the neck. Before I knew it, Joel was completely naked and ready to be soaped down. I hesitated and fumbled with a little towel.

In the morning, we discovered one difference between us. For Joel a breakfast with tough, German bread, cheese and jam is an article of faith. For me, breakfast was the meal I usually skipped altogether.

"That won't do," Joel said, as he searched my kitchen for bread, butter and cheese.

He found two slices of double soft Japanese white bread in the freezer. Hiding his horror as best he could, he put the bread into the toaster and promptly burned it. As he was scraping the coal off the bread, the bread jumped into the dishpan. The only substitute I could offer now was *mochi,* a gooey rice cake. Not a good start. But in time, I came to adjust to his strict regimen of never leaving home without a typical German breakfast. Later when we were visiting with my brother's family in Japan, Joel would eat his first typical Japanese breakfast without batting an eyelash. That made a deep impression upon my sister-in-law who had gone to some extra length to "test" this new *gaijin* family member's tolerance for dried fish and *natto,* a brown, vicious concoction of fermented soybeans and raw eggs.

"How did you manage to eat *natto?*" I asked.

"Easy. I hypnotized myself to think that I was eating peanut butter," he answered.

"He is the first and only *gaijin* who has eaten everything I served," said my sister-in-law.

One day Joel asked, "Would you like to come to Europe with me this coming summer?"

My earlier trip flashed through my mind. That trip to Europe had finished off my first marriage.

I called my friend, Ilca, that night to get her opinion and advice.

"Of course, GO! Life is too short!" was her response.

When I explained to Joel why I hesitated, he said: "All the more reason to come with me. I have a few good friends and relatives left there. They will love to meet you and I feel very comfortable being with you."

On Christmas Eve Joel's whole family gathered at his house. I was invited. There was curiosity on both sides, but it was muted and natural. No one quizzed me or asked leading questions. With one exception, the Filipino wife of Joel's nephew, I was immersed in Germans, but I was not surrounded.

Joel's mother walked in the door on the arm of her exceptionally good-looking grandson, hugged me and said, "Welcome to my family. I always wanted a daughter."

The family was of the hugging kind—a gesture I had to get used to quickly as one brother after another arrived and lifted me up in his arms. Privately, they went out of their way to tell me how much they appreciated my making their oldest brother happy.

"My brother is in good hands," said Peter, the next youngest brother.

20

Trial By Travel

"Travel together and thou shalt see." See what? See if you can stand each other under pressure.

Arriving in Bremen, we were met at the airport by Joel's friends, Wilfrid and Alfred Gies. Joel had arranged to spend a few days at their country farming and forestry estate to get over jet lag. The Gieses took the problem of jet lag and our presumed need for privacy very literally. They drove us to their summerhouse, barely showed us around and left quickly. We were left to discover a car at our disposal in front of the door, a freshly baked cherry cake on the dining room table, and a refrigerator stocked with groceries.

As it happened, jet lag was not a problem. We were up early. Joel suggested that we start the day with a barefoot walk on the grass wet and cold with dew. Why barefoot? This is part of a *Kneipp Kur*. I learned that the German Dr. Sebastian Kneipp, born in 1848, had developed a healing method based on treating a wide variety of illnesses with the judicious application of water. Outside Germany, Dr. Kneipp is virtually unknown. In

Germany, his name and method are part and parcel of the extensive health care system with its infinite number of sanitariums spread all over the country supported by national health insurance.

At that time, I was suffering from my post auto accident rheumatoid arthritis. For more than fifteen years, my doctor had routinely prescribed cortisone to control the pain and to keep me mobile. Still, in the morning, Joel had to pull me along to get me going. From the beginning, he questioned my taking cortisone on a regular and long-term basis.

When we got home, he said, "We'll begin dosing down and see what happens. We will also do *Kneipp*."

Both did small wonders for me. After our return, I was off cortisone within two weeks. *Kneipp* meant alternating between our hot Jacuzzi and cool, or even cold pool.

"Cold pool?" I thought. "This must be crazy."

But within days I was used to it.

Another thing Joel noticed when we first started eating together was the high salt content of a typical Japanese diet.

"That," he said, "cannot be good for arthritis."

As I weaned myself from cortisone, so did we dose down the salt intake. For more than ten years now, I have been free of pain and fully mobile without medication.

Back to Bremen. Here we spent an afternoon with the extended family of one of Joel's sisters-in-law, Paula. It started with a typically German *Kaffeeklatsch* for which our hostesses had spent their morning baking half a dozen stupendous cakes and tortes.

I thought, "How beautiful. But I don't eat sweets."

That was endlessly puzzling for everyone around the huge table. They agonized about this as though it were a serious handicap or illness.

"Is there something wrong with her," they asked Joel.

"No, not really," he told them.

"Well then, she must try the raspberry biscuit."

"No, please don't …"

"Ok, here's a piece of cherry cheese torte. Now that can't hurt."

I could hear and sense their concern, but I could not understand a word they were saying. I felt awkward, until one of the women, another sister-in-law, Helga, spoke up in English.

Trying to make me feel more comfortable, she said, "I had a Chinese uncle who made a lasting impression on me because his skin was so yellow. My aunt had met him when she was very young. He knew only three German words, *"Schnell ins Bett!"*—(quick to bed).

After a week of easy living, we embarked upon our train journey flashing our Eurail passes. Copenhagen was next. We had heard all our lives how civilized the Scandinavian countries were. Copenhagen confirmed our expectations. As we would do in other cities later, we went on a city bus tour. Joel noticed that the guide gave different explanations in different languages. In English, the lady would explain in some detail the horrors visited on Denmark by the German invaders during World War II. In German, many of those details were missing.

When asked about this at the end of the tour, her answers were evasive, "Sometimes it is better not to be too historically correct."

We tried to get the obligatory photo of the Mermaid and us. That was not easy. The poor maid was literally covered with Chinese tourists.

From Copenhagen the train took us through East Germany to Berlin. This was shortly after the two German states had been reunited. The massive rebuilding of East Germany had not started. Crossing from Denmark, a country of beautifully built and well kept houses and intensely green, rich farmland, it was an almost physical shock to see the unrelentingly sooty gray facades of houses everywhere. In many of the train stations we passed through, the walls showed bullet scars left from the war 45 years ago. Even the crops growing in mid summer looked anemic compared to those we had just seen in Denmark.

As our train approached Greater Berlin, it began making stops at a number of substations. Unbeknownst to us, at each station cars in the back of the train were disconnected. When we pulled into Bahnhof Tiergarten at very slow speed, ours was the only car left behind the engine. This is how Christiane and Filippo, who were to meet us, missed us. With our suitcases in front of the station, we found ourselves in a sea of non-Germans, *Ausländer,* as the Germans call them, mostly young men. Horror stories from the news sprang up in the back of our minds. While Joel went to look for his friends, I spread myself over our luggage as best I could, trying to look fierce. Our friends were waiting forlornly each with one rose in hand. They had, in fact, watched our truncated train limp into the station, but did not take it for the international train coming from Copenhagen. In their very used car, we were delivered to our hotel on Kurfürstendam, only steps away from the famous ruin of the Gedächtniskirche.

We explored the city by tour bus. Within minutes we were crossing what had, until a few months before, been the infamous wall dividing the city into East and West Berlin, the latter surrounded by the Democratic Republic of Germany (DDR). Our tour guide, a middle-aged woman from East Berlin, with good posture and a stern expression, explained the attractions, but the strain of pointing out and explaining the cultural and architectural achievements of the former Communist regime was palpable. To Western eyes much of what she was showing us was modest at best—and negligible, if not laughable, at worst.

There was one exception, the Pergamon Museum, a first-rate museum by any standards. Before you get to its impressive treasures, however, you have to get past *die Toiletten Frau*. This is a lady at the back of the entrance lobby who, in the manner of a drill sergeant, directs men to the left and women to the right and hands over one piece of toilet paper per supplicant.

"*Zwei D-Mark bitte schön!*"

"*Für was, bitte?*"

"*Seife und Handtücher!*"

The first thing you notice as you enter the toilets—no soap, no towels.

We passed Checkpoint Charlie, where Joel had crossed into East Berlin as a GI on leave many years before. We saw people standing in long lines in many places. Our guide explained that they were waiting to exchange now worthless East German money into the West German Deutschmark that was to be the currency of the reunited nation. This generous move by the West German government eventually came to be bitterly resented by those West Germans who felt that their East German brethren were given an undeserved handout.

When the cement and brick wall dividing the city of Berlin for 28 years had come down, there was one place all East Berliners wanted to go to and all, it seemed, at the same time—the KaDeWe, *Kaufhaus des Westerns*, Department Store of the West. Within hours of the fall of the wall, the place was mobbed. What was so attractive? We found the *KaDeWe* to be the ultimate in Western opulence and conspicuous mass consumption. For example, a bread section occupies most of one whole floor and features hundreds of different kinds of bread and rolls. The same holds true for the sausage and cheese sections. The store includes a whole floor of books.

All across Germany, big summer sales were on and Berlin, up and down the Kurfürstendamm, was no exception. Service was excellent. At Peek & Cloppenburg, Joel walked up to one of the well dressed salesmen and asked for black trousers. The clerk looked him over briefly, disappeared for a moment before returning with an armful of pants to try out. Every one of them fit. Another minute and Joel had found a three-piece suit. The clerk then collected the purchases and said all would be ready to be picked up at the downstairs cashier. By the time we got there, suit and pants had been packaged and were ready to go.

One night from the roof garden of our hotel, we watched the whole city explode with ecstasy among the Germans and mortal grief among the Italian "guests" over the outcome of an international soccer match. One day, Kurfürstendamm and all the side streets around our hotel were blocked by a massive, joyful gay pride parade.

In Munich, Pomseline, Joel's 82-year-old friend, met us at the station. In my mind I saw a little old lady with a cane, perhaps. Scanning the platform we noticed a large luggage dolly shooting towards us against the flow of disembarking passengers. That was Pomseline coming to gather us up. With our entire luggage in her tiny car, she drove us stick-shift through Munich traffic to her charming home on the 7th floor of a modern high-rise apartment tower in the middle of Schwabing, the artists' colony of the city. Pomseline had arranged for an energetic exploration of some of Munich's attractions. They included the *Englische Garten*, a large park running through a good part of the city. In good weather, people spend quality time here drinking huge amounts of quality beer served by Amazon waitresses carrying a dozen one liter steins supported by industrial strength bosoms. The three of us ordered one stein, but were not able to get past the half empty mark.

South of Munich towards the Alps is considered one of the loveliest spots in the world. An outing to Berchtesgaden gave us a taste of it. We hiked into the hills.

"Can you still walk?" Pomseline kept inquiring, always a few steps ahead of us glancing backwards regularly to make sure we were still in sight.

Americans have this reputation in Germany that their legs are atrophied from driving or being driven everywhere. On the way, we passed other wanderers in *lederhosen* and felt hats with little duck feathers fluttering in the wind.

"*Grüß Gott!*" they said as they passed.

We were, indeed, in what must be one of God's favorite places. At every crossing, crucifixes in stone enclosures reminded the hiker not to forget. Cow bells wafting across the meadows in full bloom completed the idyll. We were walking on well-worn and well-kept paths in a natural setting that had been carefully domesticated and maintained over many centuries, quite unlike the unkempt thicket or virgin woods of American National parks. Rustic, in Bavaria, means reaching after no more than an hour's hike a wonderfully comfortable *Gasthaus*, where the menu tempts one with bratwurst or wiener schnitzel and, always, beer.

We stopped at Schloß Linderhof. Joel had been there as a teenager on an Alpine hike with his high school teacher. At that time, the group had slept in *Heustadls*, primitive hay barns. When they visited the Schloss they had been the only visitors. Now we drove up to an enormous parking lot jammed with tour busses, where flashing signals directed us into ticket lines divided by languages. King Ludwig II, who was considered crazy by his contemporaries, built the castle and a number of others. His death is shrouded in mystery. His legacy of castles, now owned and maintained by the state of Bavaria, have all become major tourist attractions and a source of income for the state. We made a mental note never to visit any of them again.

Virtually all German cities hold open-air markets in their centers once or twice a week. Munich does it daily. It is called *der Viktualienmarkt,* and it is deservedly famous. The displays of everything edible are endless and the atmosphere is one of celebration. The Germans, I found, have much to celebrate. They live in clean, well managed cities in solidly constructed, well maintained housing. They are all covered by health insurance. In every other way, their standard of living is one of the highest in the world spread broadly among the whole population including large numbers of foreign immigrants or temporary guest workers. Yet, there is a mood of foreboding. Our friends would readily admit that they were fairly well off, protected and provided for. But their expectations for the future were almost universally fearful. This is a part of German culture I could identify with. Low expectations for the future are also part of life in Japan. I had almost forgotten about this. In America, the moods and myths are of hope and high expectations for a better future. And, since that had by now, worked out so well for me, I had internalized it more than I realized.

In Vienna Joel's stepfather and his third wife were awaiting in a two-room mansard apartment. As I already mentioned, there had been several divorces in his family, but everyone involved had stayed on friendly and civilized terms. Fritjof speaks fluent English and so does his wife Sylvia—a relief. Together we toured some of the city sampling some of the schnitzels to which the town gave its name. In one of the magnificent gilded concert halls, we attended a performance of Viennese standard pieces, sung by a Japanese coloratura in flawless German. If she can do it, maybe I can, I thought. Maybe later. It did, however, remind me of the impression I had made on Joel's mother when we were in the car on our way to a family New Year's Eve celebration. I sang German folksongs in German.

My mother-in-law to-be turned to Joel and said, "You didn't tell me that she was fluent in German!"

I had memorized the songs in school in Japan. I could sing them, but I had no idea what I was singing.

With Fritjof, who had formerly worked for an American company throughout Communist Eastern Europe, we "did" a little bit of Budapest. Much had changed since the collapse of the Soviet Union, but some things were still the same, for example, the long entrenched concept of what service should or should not be in an egalitarian Communist society. At the famous Gellert Hotel on the Danube River, we walk through the empty lobby to the marble reception counter. An elegantly dressed young lady looks up briefly. Then nothing. We wait. And wait some more. Fritjof asks if we could please sign in. Nothing. Fritjof gets the management to intervene on our behalf and finally we are handed our room keys. No explanation, no apology. Under Socialist Communism the idea of service was not important, being equal among equals was. We found remnants of this rule and the behavior it engendered in restaurants, shops, department stores and also in the Gellert's famous labyrinthine baths.

But there was also another side to this. On our second day, a young taxi driver attached himself to us. He made us an offer we could not refuse and then drove us wherever we wanted to go, or he thought we must go. We became friends and Joel, as he is apt to do, exchanged addresses and phone numbers. I had visions of this taxi driver and girl friend coming to America to stay with us for good.

Switzerland, like the Scandinavian countries, has a reputation for being one of the most civilized nations in the world, and one whose neutrality during times of war has been respected for perhaps two centuries or more. We had no cause to doubt Swiss civility. Our hotel window at the Störche in Zurich opened on the end of the Limat River, where a surprising variety of ducks frolicked in aviaries lined up along the riverbank. We took the slow post boat to Rapperswill. Here we had our first Swiss meal, *geschnetzeltes*—thin pieces of veal in a fine white sauce served over rice on exquisite plates.

As we finished our plate, dabbing up the last of the sauce with baguettes as is the custom, Joel said, "For once, this was just the right portion, don't you think? Not too much."

At this very moment the waitress approached our table with two more plates of exactly the same dish in the same quantity we had just eaten.

One of Joel's favorite cities and one of those where he has some serious roots is Baden-Baden. This is where Mäggi, his first wife, had been a longtime radio personality at the Südwestfunk, one of Germany's major network stations. We moved in with Gerda Leppert, Joel and Mäggi's "family" in Baden-Baden. Gerda, a mother type incarnate, took me to her ample bosom like a long lost daughter. But more extraordinary hospitality was to come my way. No sooner had the word got out that we had arrived, when one of Mäggi's former colleagues, Jutta, swung into action to arrange a meeting of the old labyrinthine clique.

I tried to demur, "I know none of Mäggi's old friends, and none of them know me. You go, I'll skip this one."

Jutta would have none of it. Within minutes of learning that I did not want to come, she arrived and, with arms akimbo, delivered a categorical invitation, "You absolutely must come."

What would I do? What would I say to Mäggi's lifelong friends? Origami. I would teach them the Japanese art of creating cranes, the symbol of long life and good health. Before they knew what was happening to them, I had them all lined up around a long table in a rustic, elegant country inn, folding colored paper with childlike pride into tiny souvenirs.

Joel had told me before we came to Baden-Baden, that Mäggi's legacy to him was her circle of exceptional friends. He had stayed in touch with all of them, and I could see why. They were like family, and, to my utter amazement, I was now part of that family, too. There was a warmth and openness that moved me to tears. Like when Frau Rose Mann dropped by unannounced with a bouquet of roses, which she could barely hold with two arms. Her butler carried a self-made apple pie made after a recipe, I later learned, from the *Kochbuch der Frau Rose*.

By the time we reached Idar-Oberstein, formerly famous worldwide for its diamond cutting industry, and home of Joel's sister-in-law, Else, we felt we had passed the compatibility test. But there was a slight difference of opinion when it came to formalizing our relationship. To Joel our being and staying together was a done deal and had been so from the first time we met. I had come to feel the same way, but thought a little engagement ring would be nice, too. I wanted something to show to my family and friends, who had all resigned themselves to my remaining single.

Else's family had been in the diamond business. She still had connections. What we picked is not the ordinary stand out and in your face engagement ring that challenges you to guess the carats. Mine is flat with nine little diamonds, arranged to remind me of a turtle, another symbol of longevity in Japan. Three times three also happens to be the ritual Japanese exchange of sips out of the same *sake* cups a couple takes to declare themselves married.

Before we get to the lovely Belgian city of Brugge, our next to last destination, I have to step back for a moment to explain why, on our zigzag tour of Europe, it had been included in our itinerary.

My friend, Marguerite Caliouw, had told me categorically, "If you go to Europe, you must go to Brugge!"

I met Margot, as she was called, when I was teaching Japanese at the Montebello Congregational Church in 1961. I was watching my students during recess when a woman walked up to me, introduced herself and said that she wanted to learn Japanese. She was in the import-export business and frequently made trips to Japan. We agreed that I should come to her house for private lessons. On my first visit, it became clear that Margot was not interested in learning Japanese, but looking for a friend. A lifelong friendship did develop. Margot, who was in her fifties, had never been married. I became her "adopted daughter." Our relationship had its ups and downs. Margot loved me in a selfish and possessive way. But she trusted me. Eventually, as her health declined, I became her guardian. From her bed in a nursing home, she implored me to make the trip she had dreamed of making herself before she died. She directed us to a niece in Brugge, whom she loved, and the Memmling Museum. We had to see both and report back to her.

In Brugge, our taxi driver delivered us to The Swan Hotel, one of city's finest, tucked away in a row of houses along one of the tree-shaded canals. Brugge, we had read in our brochures, was once called the Venice of he North.

"Might you suggest a good restaurant?" we asked the driver as he whisked our luggage inside.

"You got the best in town right in your hotel," he called back over his shoulder.

Our room, slightly overstuffed with exquisite furniture, offered a lovely view of the canal through Belgian lace curtains. The view and lace curtains made clear to us that a touch of class was called for if we were to have dinner in-house. In our least creased traveler's best and with good posture we walked into the restaurant looking for a good table. No problem. We were the only guests.

As we were sitting down for dinner the maitre d' in tuxedo and white gloves recommended the "romantic dinner for two." Not knowing what lay ahead, we ordered champagne cocktails for openers. The right thing for a couple on their pre-wedding honeymoon.

The dinner started with appetizers brought out by a small platoon of servers including a sommelier, waiters in tuxedos and waitresses in floor length basic black. They were dressed to kill and almost succeeded. The sommelier reappeared with every course opening a new bottle of fine wine. We lost track of the number of courses, but I felt compelled to try to empty each new bottle of wine. By about the third course I began to flag.

There were long pauses between each course. After two hours, the waiter announced that we had visitors waiting in the lobby. Joel went to meet Margot's niece and husband. Should they wait until we were finished with our romantic dinner? The maitre d' made clear that to speed up our dinner would seriously, possibly irreparably, hurt the feelings of the chef. This being Europe and all of us on our best behavior, we agreed to meet the next morning. After another two hours of courses of minute portions served artistically arranged on gigantic plates of the finest China, all accompanied by new bottles of wine, we staggered up the dimly lit but tastefully carpeted stairs to our room.

Our last stop was Paris. I had been there in strained circumstances, as I mentioned before. Joel had not been there. Fritjof had made the reservation at the Grand Hotel Jeanne D'Arc.

Our taxi wound its way through the narrow streets of the Marais district and stopped in front of what looked like just another row house crammed in between a long line of others. The owner and receptionist checked and could not find our reservation. With Joel's limited French, he persuaded the owner to call Fritjof in Vienna to find out what happened. Fritjof said he sent the check. The owner claimed he never got it. A compromise was reached, but the owner was not amused and made it very clear that he was not. We got a mansard room with a little window that allowed us late at night to watch the x-rated TV programs in a mansard across the street. In the intense heat we took turns sitting in cold water in the bath tub and draped wet towels over us on the bed.

We had been warned about pickpockets, but up to then had not experienced any trouble. Now on our first excursion into the famed Paris Métro we got stuck behind each other in the turnstile, or so I thought. In reality there was a man behind me and between us, who reached around me for my purse and tried to open it. A young woman on the other side of the turnstile screamed to warn me. The man dove under the rail, ran up to this Good Samaritan, slapped her across the face and disappeared in the crowd rushing towards the platforms.

On the whole, heat and all, this, my second visit to Paris was unquestionably more pleasant than my first one. I was now sipping wine on the Champs Elysee, slurping raw oysters at the gorgeous *Place de Voges*. This small architectural jewel was in walking distance from our hotel. We went there regularly to just sit on a bench under the old trees or visit the home of Victor Hugo, fantasizing about his life with wife and mistress under one roof. We took the Métro to *La Defénse*, the totally planned, totally modern housing and office complex. As you approach this neighborhood from the Métro, a large arch dominates the view. Looking towards Paris from its roof platform, one sees at the other end of an enormous city canyon the old and familiar Arc de Triomphe. We did our share of Museums and major sights, for which Joel has a limited capacity. What he really likes to do in European cities is just walk. Just to BE there.

21

The Soul of a Three-Year-Old Will Last 100 Years

◆

Mitsugo No Tamashii Hyaku Made

As I look out my window with a view of the Santa Monica Mountains on one side and the Pacific Ocean on the other, growing up in Japan seems like a hundred years ago. Could I have been that girl in Perfect Liberty school uniform, tight braids and an even tighter, regimented life? Could my soul still be the same and lasting till I reach 100? The answer is a matter of perspective and of who is asking the question. For older generation Japanese in both Japan and the United States, I am thoroughly Americanized. Perhaps too much so. I do not bow as readily and deeply as I was raised to do. I do not serve my husband hand and foot as would be expected of a good Japanese wife. I am comfortable in the company of men and speak my mind freely, instead of huddling with the women gossiping in the kitchen. I make my own decisions without deferring constantly to crisscrossing authorities around me—all very un-Japanese behavior from the traditional Japanese stand point.

For an American observer, namely my husband Joel, distinct remnants of typically Japanese behavior are apparent. There is, for example, *giri,* the invisible but life-defining code of obligations and reciprocals mentioned before and spelled out in mesmerizing detail by Ruth Benedict in her insightful *The Chrysanthemum and the Sword.* It is true, to this day I have difficulty accepting a gift from family members, friends or colleagues or anyone, without my brain automatically tallying up the price of the gift and making ready for a reciprocal gesture of equal value. I never go back to Japan to visit relatives and friends without carrying an extra suitcase full of gifts, which I then distribute in anticipation of their hospitality. The reverse is true for those relatives and friends when they come to visit here. They all arrive like Santa Claus, irrespective of the time of the year.

I have mentioned also the difficulty for Japanese to express wishes or demands clearly and directly. Terms like "I want you to do …" are not part of the Japanese way of polite speech. At the same time, expectations one has of what others should or should not do or say are high. If those unspoken expectations are not met, disappointments and smoldering resentments are rife. I am working on this, but am somewhat stymied by my husband's instinctive attentiveness.

Every semester my students, who come from many different countries, ask me, "What is your nationality?"

My standard short answer is, "I am Chinese by birth, Japanese by heritage and mother language, American by choice."

That leaves out, of course, the matter of culture in a more fundamental way and raises the question whether there are, indeed, fundamental differences. And, if there are, if it is possible to pick and choose, so to speak which ones one would like to keep and nurture throughout one's life, and which to adopt or discard.

Japanese and Asian cultures have natural similarities in their underlying ethical concepts though emphases vary. A good person in Western cultures is one who is respectful to his elders, sensitive to those around him and compassionate to those less fortunate. In Western culture, the Protestant Work Ethic teaches that hard work, honesty and loyalty will be rewarded and are the basis for a good life and possibly pleasing to God. All of this, with the exception of possibly pleasing one God, is also true for Japanese culture with one fundamental difference. In Western culture a good person in the above sense can enjoy considerable freedom of choice. In fact, upon my coming to America, I found the choices suddenly open all around me almost overwhelming. In Japanese culture I had been taught and knew my "proper station." I was brought up to be a good person safely surrounded by ironclad rules of hierarchy and obligations. This is precisely why I had to plan my "escape" in secrecy and, when it was finally revealed, cover it with plausible, though in reality false, explanations.

It is possible that some of the cultural differences are becoming muted by the instantaneous globalization of information. I have noticed that some of the extreme formalities among my Japanese family and friends show signs of loosening up among the younger generation. Still, we bow and bow, but rarely touch or hug. I am uncomfortable if students address me by my first name. I find it impossible to do likewise with my professional superiors or former teachers.

I would like to believe that I have learned to be selective, to pick and choose, so to speak, the best from two cultures, two worlds; but early cultural programming is hard to overcome. I still speak in a different voice when I talk to Japanese family or friends. I can never completely suppress my urge to bow even before my mother. My feelings are hurt if my sister tells me that I'm selfish, and Japanese culture won't let me respond in kind until later, after some *sake* has opened the floodgates holding back our little sibling resentments.

When I am in Japan, where all my relatives and friends are now well off, and the war and postwar calamities are a distant memory for the survivors and thus pure history for the following generation, I am often asked if I could live in Japan again, or whether I had plans to return to spend my old age there. My answer to the former is technically yes, my answer to the latter is no.

When I took flight as a 19-year-old to come to the land of freedom and opportunity, I had high hopes of escaping the suffocating constraints of Japanese society of the mid 20th Century. I did not land in a bed of roses. The freedoms were there but I had to fight for them every step of the way. My hopes were not dashed. My dreams of an independent life came true.

Now, together we can all just BE there in our lives, too. My favorite poem from Sanskrit sums it up:

> Look to this Day.
> For it is life, the very life of life.
> In its brief course lie all the varieties and realities
> Of your existence.
> The Bliss of Growth, The Glory of Action, The Splendor of
> Beauty.
> For yesterday is already a dream,
> And tomorrow is only a vision;
> But today well lived, makes every yesterday a dream of happiness,
> And every tomorrow a vision of hope.
> Look well, therefore, to this Day.
> Such is the salutation of the Dawn.
> ~ *From the Sanskrit* ~

About the Author

Kaori Tanegashima and her husband Joel Busch, a professor of political science, live in Pacific Palisades, California, where they enjoy the sun and the ocean. Both look back happily on a lifetime of teaching as they approach the process of retiring.

Kaori is looking forward to having more time for her long-time hobby of painting and for her recent challenge of mastering the harp. Both have sung in the Brentwood-Palisades Chorale with the Palisades Symphony Orchestra for many years.

Their plans include tutoring students from many different countries in English as a Second Language and visiting family and friends in Japan, Germany and Canada.

Notes on the Photos

Front book cover:

> Upper left—Kaori's ancestors: grandfather, grandmother and mother as a young lady.

> Middle right—Kaori at 17 in Kobe harbor dreaming of going to America

> The rifle is a Tanegashima musket (arquebus). Photo courtesy of: Monte Schumacher (www.trocadero.com/MONTES)

Preface:

> In this re-enactment the Portuguese captain demonstrates the power of the arquebus to Lord Tokitaka Tanegashima.

> Kaori's passport at age 19 marks the beginning of her adventures in a new world.

Chapter 1:

> Kaori's family: Mother, father, older sisters Fusako and Michiko and older brother Keiji.

Chapter 3:

Family photo with two new members, step-mother Masako and baby sister, Megumi. Kaori, age 12, is on the left.

Chapter 4:

—Kaori in Perfect Liberty High School uniform.

—Playing baseball with the boys

—Kaori as captain of the Ping Pong Club in PL High School

Chapter 5:

—The Steamship Santosu-maru as it leaves Kobe Harbor April 2, 1960

—Farewell cherry blossoms!

—Goodbye and bon voyage from somber friend and family

—Ayako and Kaori with the ship's captain at the captain's table

—Two overnight singing sensations aboard ship

Chapter 7:

—Kaori the art major and sculptress

—In cap and gown for A.A. degree

—Official portrait in cap and gown and B. A. degree

Chapter 10:

—Hustling along with classmates for her M.A. degree

Chapter 13:

—Kaori in her very own two story townhouse

Chapter 14:

—Kaori, Japanese language teacher to the Monkees, with two of her favorite students (Peter Tolk on the right).

Chapter 16:

—The newest U.S. Citizen—Kaori Tanegashima.

978-0-595-49914-4
0-595-49914-7

Printed in the United States
134700LV00004B/6/P

9 780595 499144